Alan Titchmarsh
how to garden

Pests and Problems

Pests and Problems

BOOKS

10 9 8 7 6 5 4 3 2 1

Published in 2011 by BBC Books, an imprint of
Ebury Publishing, a Random House Group Company

The Random House Group Limited Reg. No. 954009

Addresses for companies within the Random House
Group can be found at **www.randomhouse.co.uk**

The Random House Group Limited
supports The Forest Stewardship
Council (FSC), the leading
international forest certification
organisation. All our titles that are
printed on Greenpeace approved
FSC certified paper carry the FSC
logo. Our paper procurement
policy can be found at www.
rbooks.co.uk/environment

FSC
www.fsc.org
MIX
Paper from
responsible sources
FSC™ C004592

A CIP catalogue record for this book is available from
the British Library.

ISBN 978 1 84 607406 6

Produced by OutHouse!
Shalbourne, Marlborough, Wiltshire SN8 3QJ

BBC BOOKS
COMMISSIONING EDITOR: Lorna Russell
PROJECT EDITOR: Caroline McArthur
PRODUCTION: Phil Spencer

OUTHOUSE!
COMMISSIONING EDITOR: Sue Gordon
SERIES EDITOR: Polly Boyd
SERIES ART DIRECTOR: Robin Whitecross
CONTRIBUTING EDITOR: Jo Weeks
EDITOR: Candida Frith-Macdonald
DESIGNER: Sharon Cluett
ILLUSTRATIONS by Lizzie Harper,
Susan Hillier, Janet Tanner
PHOTOGRAPHS by Jonathan Buckley except where
credited otherwise on page 128
CONCEPT DEVELOPMENT & SERIES DESIGN:
Elizabeth Mallard-Shaw, Sharon Cluett

Colour origination by Altaimage, London
Printed and bound by Firmengruppe APPL,
Wemding, Germany

Contents

Introduction

Gardening is one of the best and most fulfilling activities on earth, but it can sometimes seem complicated and confusing. The answers to problems can usually be found in books, but big fat gardening books can be rather daunting. Where do you start? How can you find just the information you want without wading through lots of stuff that is not appropriate to your particular problem? Well, a good index is helpful, but sometimes a smaller book devoted to one particular subject fits the bill better – especially if it is reasonably priced and if you have a small garden where you might not be able to fit in everything suggested in a larger volume.

The *How to Garden* books aim to fill that gap – even if sometimes it may be only a small one. They are clearly set out and written, I hope, in a straightforward, easy-to-understand style. I don't see any point in making gardening complicated, when much of it is based on common sense and observation. (All the key techniques are explained and illustrated, and I've included plenty of tips and tricks of the trade.)

There are suggestions on the best plants and the best varieties to grow in particular situations and for a particular effect. I've tried to keep the information crisp and to the point so that you can find what you need quickly and easily and then put your new-found knowledge into practice. Don't worry if you're not familiar with the Latin names of plants. They are there to make sure you can find the plant as it will be labelled in the nursery or garden centre, but where appropriate I have included common names, too. Forgetting a plant's name need not stand in your way when it comes to being able to grow it.

Above all, the *How to Garden* books are designed to fill you with passion and enthusiasm for your garden and all that its creation and care entails, from designing and planting it to maintaining it and enjoying it. For more than fifty years gardening has been my passion, and that initial enthusiasm for watching plants grow, for trying something new and for just being outside pottering has never faded. If anything I am keener on gardening now than I ever was and get more satisfaction from my plants every day. It's not that I am simply a romantic, but rather that I have learned to look for the good in gardens and in plants, and there is lots to be found. Oh, there are times when I fail – when my plants don't grow as well as they should and I need to try harder. But where would I rather be on a sunny day? Nowhere!

The *How to Garden* handbooks will, I hope, allow some of that enthusiasm – childish though it may be – to rub off on you, and the information they contain will, I hope, make you a better gardener, as well as opening your eyes to the magic of plants and flowers.

Preventing problems

It is, perhaps, inevitable that some plants will suffer health problems from time to time, but it is rare that a well-tended garden is riddled with pests and diseases. There are plenty of measures that you can take to prevent problems in the first place and to ensure your plants are healthy enough either to fend them off or to recover quickly if they are attacked. Often, it is simply a matter of understanding what they need to grow well and realizing when and why they might not be getting it.

Understanding nature

Nature knows what she's doing and does it very well. But we gardeners have a tendency to meddle with nature, which can sometimes lead to problems. So, where nature would have a couple of forest trees, some tough, shrubby undergrowth and a few hardy bulbs and perennials, gardeners want maples from America, roses from China and lavender from the Mediterranean. And we want them all looking perfect, all the time.

Fortunately, we can have a range of beautiful plants in our gardens, and they can grow very well, but the price we pay is that we have to work to keep them healthy. Some are not fully adapted to local conditions, such as climate or soil type, or they may not be resistant to indigenous pests and diseases – even those that are can suffer some damage. In addition, many of the plants we now grow in our gardens have been genetically modified by selective breeding, which can sometimes make them more vulnerable to problems. For example, the big, blowsy flowers of some modern bedding varieties are much more likely to be damaged by heavy rain than the smaller blooms of their more primitive ancestors.

Our native mountain ash (*Sorbus aucuparia*) grows naturally on exposed mountains and hillsides, in poor or shallow soils with low fertility. Perfectly adapted to our conditions, it is a tough plant that suffers very few pests or diseases.

Gardens are unnatural

Along with all these factors, there is the final, inescapable fact that gardens are not natural. They have areas of bare earth for flowers, shrubs and vegetables, and patches of open ground where only a few species of plant – grasses – are supposed to grow. Then there are paths and patios, and hedgerows and fences. Nowadays, most gardeners try hard to garden with nature in mind, but even the most naturalistic gardens have been artificially manufactured and need to be carefully managed.

By now you've probably got the idea that gardeners are like King Canute, hopelessly holding back a tide of pests and diseases and other problems, but this isn't the case. Luckily, nature is also very adaptable and forgiving. The wide range of non-native flowers we grow are assiduously pollinated by our bees, resident birds flit happily through the boughs of exotic trees, and frogs, toads, ladybirds and ground beetles find food among the leaves and debris of plants from as far afield as Chile, Japan and Australia.

Don't forget

Plant breeders are still aiming to produce better floral displays, but in addition many are working towards making plants more resistant to diseases.

Canna lilies come from tropical regions of America and Asia, where they grow on forest edges. In our cool, temperate climate, they need a sunny spot to flower well and are unlikely to survive a cold winter outdoors.

Get nature on your side

One of the most important steps you can take towards avoiding problems in your garden is to establish a healthy ecosystem. Put very simply, ecosystems are communities of organisms that live together, something like a family. Where the ecosystem is healthy, it is balanced, which means individual organisms – in this case pests – are less likely to take over. In other words, you have a happy family.

To create a thriving ecosystem, you need to make the garden an attractive place for the creepy-crawlies, birds, hedgehogs and other creatures that do such a good job of clearing up the bad guys for you. For example, if you encourage birds into your garden, they will eat insect pests such as aphids, caterpillars and weevils. This saves you having to go out and pick these blighters off your favourite plants or resort to spraying unpleasant chemicals. You should also grow a range of plants of all types and sizes, so that pests and diseases are less likely to do wholesale damage.

Planting for wildlife

There are two main aims in planting for wildlife: providing food and providing habitat. One of the best ways to provide food is to choose plants that bloom over a long season. Flowers come in all shapes and sizes, and they don't have to be big and colourful to provide nectar for insects. Simply try to include very early flowerers and very late ones, as well as those that bloom during mid- to late spring and summer. This is where our habit of growing plants from all over the world comes in very useful, as it allows us to have flowers almost all the year round.

Once you've got the wildlife into the garden to eat, you can increase the chances of it staying put by providing places to nest, reproduce, roost and hibernate. Birds like to have cover, which makes them feel safer, so plant a selection of densely branched shrubs, including some evergreens as well as deciduous ones. Join the plantings together so birds don't have to risk flying into the open to get from one spot to another. Shrubby areas also provide cover and habitat for the other creatures you want in your garden. Many ground-dwelling beetles and insects, as well as shrews, toads and hedgehogs, like to live and forage among the fallen leaves and twigs.

Having a pool or pond, even if it is only small, is one of the best ways to encourage a wide range of beneficial creatures into your garden. Water also makes a good focal point and is worth having just for its decorative qualities.

Providing water

Within the main ecosystem of a garden, there should be many other smaller ecosystems and, if you have space for it, a pond or pool is one of the most important. Frogs, toads newts, dragonflies and damselflies are among the many creatures that prefer a garden with water. Most are on your side in the battle against pests, and they are all interesting cohabitees. Everyone knows that ponds can be dangerous for children, but with a little care it is possible to make them safe, and kids really love the wildlife they attract.

Gardening for wildlife

After planting and providing water, the next best way to get nature on your side is to be a less-than-tidy gardener. This doesn't mean you should allow weeds to grow or leave dead and dying plants in place. It just means you should think about having a few spots where you leave heaps of twigs and rotting leaves, areas where you don't cut down flowerheads as soon as the last petal has fallen, and places where you leave a few stones in a pile and two or three terracotta pots lying on their sides or standing on their rims. Places like these are havens for tiny insects, beetles, worms and spiders that either prey on pests or provide food for other creatures that do.

Adding variety

Planting a wide variety of trees, shrubs and low-growing plants not only provides plenty of flowers for insects to pollinate, it also helps to protect against devastation by any single pest or disease. Chemical

Companion planting

Companion planting is popular in vegetable patches and to a lesser extent in fruit gardens, and some of the principles could easily be transferred to ornamentals. The ideas behind companion planting are to group plants that like to grow together and to grow plants that deter pests among plants that seem to attract them. Research suggests it is not so much a partnership that is created, but more that mixing the plants together makes it more difficult for any pest to find its favourite target. The drawback of companion planting is that while some people have great success, others find it makes no difference at all – but it is fun to experiment!

As well as making excellent ground cover, nasturtiums are well known for their attractiveness to pests such as blackfly and cabbage white butterfly caterpillars, and may distract them from precious vegetables.

Good companions:
- Lettuce and onions
- Runner beans and carrots
- Carrots and peas
- Sweetcorn, potatoes, peas and runner beans
- Tomatoes and roses

Deterrent plants:
- Catmint (*Nepeta*) against flea beetles
- Garlic against aphids and red spider mites
- Hyssop (*Hyssopus*) and mint (*Mentha*) against cabbage white butterflies
- French marigold (*Tagetes*) against pest nematodes, slugs and wireworms
- Rosemary (*Rosmarinus*) against carrot fly
- Wormwood (*Artemisia*) against vegetable pests, particularly flea beetles

pesticides and fungicides were, for the most part, developed to deal with large-scale problems in agriculture, where crops are usually grown as monocultures. Pests and diseases find something they like and stay for the duration – they can

Don't forget

Trees are especially important in increasing numbers of birds in gardens, but they do need space. If you can fit them in, just one or two will make a difference.

survive for months or even years in such a paradise. Growing large numbers of the same plant can be a risky business, and vegetable gardens are often more badly hit by problems than ornamental gardens for this reason. In vegetable gardens, 'rotating' crops between beds helps to prevent a build-up of problems, but this is not really possible in ornamental gardens. However, it makes sense to vary where you plant particular annuals from year to year.

As far as gardeners are concerned, there are really two types of wildlife: the sort we want in our garden and the sort we don't. You can make your garden a better place for the ones you want, although some will be present anyway, but it can prove hard to deter the ones that you don't want, since they can be very persistent (for more about these *see* pages 26–7).

Frogs, toads and newts

Amphibians of all sorts love to feed on insects. All they really need is a pond with plenty of planting at the edge and on the banks and at least one sloping edge to allow access, plus a few untidy spots of leaf litter. It's best not to move eggs or tadpoles; if you have a suitable pond, the adults will find you. Frogs, toads and newts can live together, but fish will eat their eggs and young.

Bees

Many bees pollinate flowers, so they're vital in and around the fruit and vegetable garden. They usually create their own living quarters, but if you want to help, you can buy special nesting boxes for bumblebees. You can also simply bury clay flowerpots upside down or at a slight angle, with the drainage holes uncovered so that bees can get in and out.

Solitary bees prefer to live in small holes in walls or wood; bundles of twigs or short lengths of bamboo are their ideal home (*see* opposite). If you drill holes in wood to make homes for them instead, be sure to use untreated timber. The holes should be narrow, no more than 10mm (½in) across, and 10–15cm (4–6in) deep.

Blue tits and great tits will often use nesting boxes in peaceful, shady positions. Once in residence, they will forage locally for small insects and caterpillars to feed their young, which will help keep down pest populations. Set up nest boxes in spring, before the breeding season starts.

Wasps

The young of many wasp species are proficient at pest control, including those of the stinging type that are such unwelcome guests at outdoor meals. Solitary and parasitic wasps are less likely to gatecrash parties, and both have young that feed on the larvae of insects such as aphids and weevils. Some parasitic wasp species are used commercially as biological controls (*see* page 27). They lay their eggs inside larvae, pupae or eggs, and when the young hatch they consume their host.

Beetles and bugs

Many beetles are helpful to gardeners. While some of them are well known, others generally go unnoticed but still play their part.

Ladybirds are very fond of aphids. Their larvae (*see* box, opposite) are knobbly and black, with yellow-orange or white spots, and it's hard to believe that they will grow up to be as lovely as their parents. Their favourite food is also aphids, so they are very welcome in the garden. The devil's coach horse beetle is jet black and about 2.5cm (1in) long. It lives under stones and logs and preys on slugs, as well as cutworms and leatherjackets. Ground beetles also eat slugs, along with a variety of insect eggs. There are many species, the biggest being about

3.5cm (1½in) long. Tiger beetles are smaller, and it is their larvae that are most useful to gardeners, as they feed on a variety of insects. Flower (anthocorid) bugs look a little like flies with black, brown and white markings, and prey on aphids, mites and thrips.

There is little you can do to encourage beetles and bugs into the garden; they are usually there anyway. However, it is a good idea to have some 'untidy' areas for them to live in, and to avoid using pesticides, which can be indiscriminate about what they kill.

Spiders and flies

Everyone knows that spiders eat flies by trapping them in webs. They are generally unfussy about what sort of insects they eat, and dispose of a wide range of pests, as do the young of hoverflies, lacewings and tachinid flies.

Many hoverflies look a little like small, flattened wasps, but their hovering flight is very different and they lack the wasp's pinched waist. The adults feed on pollen and nectar, while their larvae eat vast numbers of aphids.

Lacewing larvae also feed on aphids and other small insects. The adults have long, lacy wings and green, brown or black bodies. Some tachinid flies are similar in appearance to a normal housefly, but there are plenty of different species and many are only a few millimetres long. Caterpillars are their speciality; the young hatch within the caterpillar, eating it from the inside.

Earthworms

Earthworms and microscopic soil-dwellers contribute to the health of your garden by breaking down dead plant material. Earthworm activity also creates tunnels in the soil, which helps with aeration and drainage. Adding plenty of organic matter to your soil will help to keep your populations of earthworms happy, and they in turn will keep your soil healthy.

Birds and small mammals

Apart from the fact that they are a pleasure to have in the garden, birds eat many pests. Blue tits, great tits, robins, swallows and martins are insect- and caterpillar-eaters, while songthrushes are partial to snails; blackbirds like the odd slug, rolled in soil to get rid of the slime. Green woodpeckers eat ants, but are very shy birds and can't be guaranteed to keep populations under control. Feeding stations regularly topped up with sunflower seeds, peanuts and other goodies help to ensure birds stay in your garden, particularly through the winter months when other food sources are scarce.

Shrews and hedgehogs eat slugs and worms, as well as small insects and beetles. Providing habitat in the form of untidy areas is the best way to ensure they live happily in your garden.

There is a multitude of creatures that will make your garden their home.

① We might find spiders a bit creepy, but they do us a real favour by living in our gardens. Not all insects that fall prey to them are garden pests, but some most definitely are.

② Mason bees and ladybirds are among the beneficial insects that love a narrow, tubular home, such as these bamboo canes and logs.

Growing conditions

It seems like a no-brainer, as they say, but one of the best ways of avoiding problems with plants is to grow the right kind – that is, those that are compatible with the conditions in your garden. Knowing your local conditions, so you can choose the types of plants that will enjoy them, is the start of successful gardening. The prevailing climate in your area is obviously important, but just as crucial is what sort of soil you have.

Your soil

Most soils are made up of varying quantities of loam, sand and clay. Depending on where you live, your soil may also contain some level of either chalk or peat.

Given the choice, most gardeners would prefer to have loamy soil. Loam is dark brown and crumbly textured. It drains well, but not too quickly, and is naturally fertile. It gives most plants the perfect conditions for healthy growth. Even those with a reputation for fussiness, such as peonies and large-flowered clematis, do well on loam.

Sandy soil is less fertile than loam and drains very well – it is often called 'light' soil because it is easy to dig. Plants that like to be dryish tend to do well on sand. There are many irises, for example, that need to be hot and dry in summer otherwise they don't flower.

Clay is a bit of a challenge to dig, being claggy when wet and hard when dry. However, it is very fertile and moisture-retentive and many plants, including roses, seem to prefer it to other soils.

Chalky soil is lighter than clay and nearly always alkaline (*see* below). It is reasonably fertile but usually stony and shallow, which means you risk digging into the subsoil when you work it. A number of plants prefer chalk, including many bellflowers (*Campanula*), echinacea and rudbeckia, as well as plenty of wildflowers, such as poppies and cornflowers. However, acid-lovers, like rhododendrons, camellias, pieris and most Japanese maples (*Acer*), suffer nutrient deficiencies (*see* page 25) and fail to thrive.

Soil pH

pH is a measurement of the acid–alkaline balance in soil. Very acidic is pH1, pH7 is neutral and pH14 is very alkaline. Most soils are somewhere in the middle of the range. pH influences the way plants take up nutrients through their roots. Some plants need acid soil in order to get all that they need, while others seem unaffected by pH.

Identifying your soil type

Whatever type of gardening you plan to do, your first step should be to find out what type of soil you have, as it has an impact on how well different plants grow. The five main types are shown here, but yours might not be clearly one or another. It's possible to have a mixture of garden soils, say peaty loam or chalky clay, or different types in one garden.

① Sandy soil feels gritty, like sand at the beach. Take a handful and it will feel light and pour out between your fingers rather than forming a ball, because it's loose-textured and usually dry.

② Clay soil feels heavy and sticky, and can be rolled into a smooth ball. It forms lumps when wet, and is hard and solid when dry.

③ Chalky soil is usually full of pale lumps of chalk, which crumble if you rub them together. The soil has a loose texture, making it easy to dig.

④ Loam is even-textured, feels soft and is a mid- to dark brown. It can be squeezed into a ball, but if it is rubbed it easily breaks into crumbs again.

⑤ Peat is very dark and open-textured, almost like a sponge. It holds onto water well, but can be rather crumbly and difficult to re-wet when it does dry out.

Many plants are remarkably unfussy and will perform well in a wide range of environments. However, there are some that are much harder to please or that are more likely to suffer from pests or diseases. It is sensible to find out as much as possible, particularly before making expensive purchases.

BULBS
Crocus

Hyacinthoides (bluebells)

Narcissus (daffodils, many)

PERENNIALS
Ajuga reptans (bugle)

Alchemilla mollis (lady's mantle)

Aquilegia (columbine)

Armeria maritima (thrift)

Erigeron karvinskianus (fleabane)

Ferns (many)

Geranium (almost any, though purple-leaved ones are less tough)

Helleborus (hellebore)

Origanum vulgare 'Aureum' (oregano)

Sedum spectabile (ice plant)

CLIMBING PLANTS
Clematis montana (other clematis can be more temperamental)

Cotoneaster horizontalis

Euonymus fortunei

Hedera (ivy)

Lonicera (honeysuckle, many)

Rambling roses (many, including 'Rambling Rector')

SHRUBS
Aucuba (spotted laurel)

Berberis

Brachyglottis, such as 'Sunshine'

Buddleja davidii (buddleia)

Cotoneaster

Heathers

Ribes sanguineum (flowering currant)

Rosa rugosa

Rosmarinus (rosemary)

Don't forget

There are very few inhabited places on earth where no plants grow. No matter how difficult conditions in your garden are, something will grow there.

Not all plants relish chalky soil, but the lovely American coneflower, *Echinacea purpurea*, with its purple, daisy-like flowers, is very happy in it.

Garden centres sell inexpensive and easy-to-use kits for testing pH.

Soil pH is quite hard to alter because of the sheer quantity of soil in any garden, and any alterations are only temporary because they get washed out by the rain. This means that gardeners who want healthy plants should choose those that like their existing pH. If you garden on alkaline soil and are keen on acid-loving plants, you may consider making raised beds and filling them with acid soil. However, there is one place where it really is worth tampering with the pH, and that's the vegetable garden. Most vegetables like neutral soil, but brassicas prefer slightly alkaline conditions. Adding compost and rotted manure to the soil – an annual event in the vegetable garden – gradually makes it slightly more acid. To counteract this, many vegetable gardeners scatter lime (which is alkaline) in the autumn.

Your situation

No matter what sort of soil you have, it will be affected by the climate and other conditions in your garden. For example, even the best-quality loam will become thin and infertile under the shade of a long-established conifer or beside a sheltering wall (*see* rain shadows, page 17), while poor underlying drainage can make even sandy soil soggy. It makes good sense to

choose plants that can survive these conditions, but you can also improve them to a certain extent by digging, fertilizing and watering (*see* pages 20–4). This will increase your planting options as well as the health of your existing plants.

While you can add shelter and shade to your garden, there is not much you can do about temperature, rain or sunshine – unless thinning or felling trees is an option with the latter – and all these should also play a part in your choice of plants. For example, a woodland plant will do best in a shady situation, and a plant that evolved to survive on windy mountainsides in the wild is better able to withstand similar conditions in your garden than one that comes from sheltered, sunny lowlands.

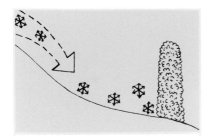

Frost pockets are often much colder than the rest of the garden and plants growing in them will be more susceptible to cold damage. Solid barriers at the foot of a slope, for instance a hedge or wall, will act as reservoirs for cold air.

Microclimates

Although your general conditions are determined by the soil and local weather, every garden has a range of microclimates – spots that are particularly sheltered or somewhat more exposed, drier or wetter and so on than the garden as a whole. Although some of these areas are a challenge, others are a positive benefit. All offer you the chance to expand your range of plants and increase your gardening knowledge.

Frost pockets

Frost pockets are places where cold air collects. They are much slower to warm up after icy weather and tend to be much quicker to cool down at night. Snow stays in a frost pocket long after it has melted elsewhere. Warm air rises and cold air sinks, so pockets are often found in valleys or dips, but they also occur in shady spots that the sun doesn't warm.

If the cold air is 'pooling' along a hedge or fence, consider making gaps to allow it to flow through. Thinning branches can improve

airflow too. Don't plant spring-flowering shrubs and trees in frost pockets, because the blossom will be damaged or killed by the cold. This is particularly important for fruit trees, since frosted flowers are unattractive to pollinating insects and your crop will be affected. The same goes for plants grown mainly for their foliage. Emerging leaves are very sensitive to the cold and may turn brown or black if frosted.

Wind and wind tunnels

You only need to look at the way the wind 'prunes' trees in coastal areas to see that windy conditions are challenging. Most plants can cope with some wind, which also has the benefit of reducing attack by pests and diseases, but if you're in a very windy area, the exposure outweighs the benefits. The best solution is to

reduce the wind's speed by erecting fencing or planting windbreaks. Any barriers must be permeable to avoid creating turbulence, which is just as damaging as wind. Look after windbreak plants well in their early years: good planting, staking and aftercare (see pages 21–4) are vital to help them withstand the wind while they establish. (For some wind-resistant plants see page 19.)

Where the wind is funnelled through narrow spaces, its potential to damage is even greater. Wind tunnels are most damaging where the wind is squeezed between solid structures, such as fences or walls. As it sweeps along the narrow space, the wind speeds up, buffeting everything in its path. Barriers are the best solution; a well-placed fencing panel or two can make all the difference.

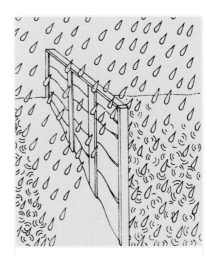

Even tough plants can be 'scorched' in a wind tunnel, because they can't take up water fast enough to counter the drying wind. Evergreens can be damaged when the ground is frozen and early flowers are at risk too. The problem is worse if the soil is shallow.

Since rain rarely falls vertically, the leeward side of fences, hedges and walls is usually dry – in a rain shadow. Despite the dry conditions, many plants still do well beside walls and fences, because they appreciate the shelter and extra warmth.

Dry soil and rain shadows

If you garden on very freely draining soil, such as sand, it is a major challenge to slow the water down enough for your plants to be able to make use of it. Add well-rotted manure or compost at least annually and every time you plant – and plant properly (*see* page 21). Water all plants well until they are fully established, and mulch thickly to prevent water evaporation. It is important to feed regularly too, because the water will take many nutrients with it as it rushes through the soil. The same advice applies where rainfall is low. Do everything you can to preserve every drop of water that falls. That includes installing water butts beside the house, garage and shed.

Even wet gardens can have rain shadows – areas sheltered from the rain that are very dry. Spots beside walls and fences and in the lee of

The climbing hydrangea (*Hydrangea anomala* subsp. *petiolaris*) is a tough plant that seems immune to the dry, shady conditions found beside north-facing walls.

Frost and wind damage

Both frost and wind can cause withered, blackened or brown leaves and young shoots. With wind damage, usually only the windward side of the plant is affected, while frost damage may be limited to the lower shoots. It's often better to move a susceptible plant than struggle to keep it in an unsuitable position. Wind can also cause 'wind rock', loosening a plant's grip in its planting hole; always stake new trees and even shrubs in vulnerable places.

trees or shrubs are typical examples. Near trees and shrubs, the effect is increased because big plants take up large quantities of water, while near walls, the dryness is often exacerbated by foundations, which can soak up water like a sponge, and by the warmer conditions created as bricks or concrete absorb heat from the sun. Pests like red spider mite love these conditions (*see* page 71).

Plant climbers and shrubs a little way out and lean climbers towards their support. Again, good planting will help them, and it's a good idea to pick plants adapted for growing in dry conditions on a sunny wall or in a tree's shade (*see* page 19).

Waterlogging and floods

Damp, boggy areas usually occur where drainage is poor or the soil is compacted. They can also be the result of a high water table or flooding. Where small areas are waterlogged on a regular basis, it is worth considering installing drains or even building raised beds to keep the plants up out of the worst of it. Double digging (*see* pages 20–1) will also help to improve drainage. Another option is to go with the flow and create a bog garden, perhaps beside a pond. Many lovely plants grow in very damp situations and plenty of wildlife thrives there.

A one-off flood that spreads through the whole garden can be devastating, destroying years of hard work in just a few days. If the waterlogging is short-lived, there is a chance that some plants will survive. If it happens in the winter, wait until spring to see the true extent of the damage. Plants are less likely to be killed by floods in the winter months than in summer, because they don't use their roots as much when dormant.

Stay off flooded soil until it is reasonably dry, otherwise you risk compacting it and compounding the problem, but once you can get into the garden do a thorough tidying-up job. Remove damaged branches and shoots and dig up plants that are obviously dead. After summer floods, apply a foliar feed as a tonic and make sure you water in dry spells. Finer roots die during waterlogging, leaving the plants much more vulnerable to drought.

If you know that your garden is prone to flooding, it is best to plant slow-maturing plants, such as trees

Building sites

Builders are renowned for leaving all sorts of rubbish behind in the ground surrounding their workplace. Their activities will also have compacted the soil and can reduce drainage to almost nothing. Even if the garden of a new build has been landscaped and planted up, the effects are probably cosmetic and the soil underneath will be in a poor state. Don't panic. Come up with a good general plan for the garden and then slowly work your way around it. Clear small areas at a time, getting rid of bricks, concrete and other rubbish and adding compost as you go. If the soil is of very poor quality, topsoil can be delivered by the lorry load, but check that it is weed-free before buying it.

and shrubs, on mounded soil. This helps the soil around them to drain quickly, so even if you lose your smaller plants to a flood, the overall structure of the garden has a better chance of survival.

Don't forget

Floodwater can contain all sorts of unpleasant pollutants, from chemicals to sewage. Do not eat vegetables that have grown in flooded soil.

A bog garden is a perfect solution for a patch of damp ground and there are many plants that simply love puddling about in mud.

Plants for a purpose

It can be hard to find plants that not only survive but also perform well in the more challenging areas in a garden. These lists should give you some help.

Many sedums thrive in shallow soil that is low in nutrients. The late-summer flowers of *Sedum* 'Herbstfreude' ('Autumn Joy') provide nectar for bees and butterflies.

For low-fertility soil

Amaranthus caudatus (p)
Buddleja davidii (s)
Centranthus ruber (p)
Crataegus (s/t)
Eschscholzia californica (a)
Glaucium flavum (b)
Lavandula (s)
Limonium platyphyllum (p)
Papaver rhoeas (a)
Tropaeolum hybrids (a)
Ulex (s)

For very shallow soil

Armeria maritima (p)
Aubrieta (p)
Campanula poscharskyana (p)
Carpobrotus edulis (p)
Cerastium tomentosum (p)
Erigeron karvinskianus (p)
Malcolmia maritima (a)
Origanum vulgare 'Aureum' (p)
Saxifraga (p)
Sedum (p)

For dry soil

Aloysia triphylla (s)
Anthemis punctata (p)
Betula (t)
Centaurea cyanus (a)
Cleome hassleriana (a)
Echinops ritro (p)
Eryngium giganteum (p)
Genista aetnensis (s)
Hibiscus rosa-sinensis (s)
Olearia (s)
Phlomis fruticosa (p)

SHADE
Aucuba (s)
Anemone nemorosa (p)
Berberis (s)
Betula (t)
Cotoneaster conspicuus (p)
Cyclamen coum (p)
Ferns, some (p)
Geranium macrorrhizum (p)
Geranium phaeum (p)
Hedera (cl)
Jasminum nudiflorum (s/cl)
Parthenocissus (cl)

For damp soil

Alnus incana (t)
Astilbe (p)
Bergenia (p)
Caltha palustris (p)
Filipendula ulmaria 'Aurea' (p)
Geum rivale (p)
Iris pseudacorus (p)
Lythrum salicaria (p)
Primula beesiana (p)
Rodgersia (p)
Salix (s/t)
Sambucus (s)

SHADE
Aconitum (p)
Ajuga (p)
Cercis siliquastrum (s/t)
Convallaria majulis (p)
Digitalis purpurea (b)
Flaeagnus (s)
Epimedium (p)
Ferns (p)
Helleborus (p)
Heuchera (p)
Lysichiton americanus (p)
Pulmonaria (p)
Viola (p)

For windy spots

Acer pseudoplatanus (t)
Brachyglottis 'Sunshine' (s)
Grasses, many (p)
Cotoneaster (s)
Griselinia littoralis (s)
Heathers (p/s)
Hebe, many (s)
Ilex (s/t)
Olearia × haastii (s)
Pinus sylvestris (t)
Sorbus aria (t)
Tamarix (s)

Good gardening techniques

Never underestimate your role in the health of your garden: from soil preparation to planting and aftercare, your plants are much more likely to survive and thrive if treated well. Garden management should be enjoyable and much of the time simply consists of making sure all is well, pulling up weeds and tying in loose stems. All plants benefit from regular attention: weeding (*see* pages 30–4), watering, feeding and pruning all help you to avoid problems, or spot them before they take hold.

Regular watering in dry weather is a vital part of your plant-care regime.

Digging

Whether you are cultivating a vegetable bed for spring sowings or making space in a border for a new acquisition, good preparation makes a huge difference to the results. Digging through the soil allows you to break up hard clumps, dislodge large stones and kill weeds, all of which will improve drainage and remove competition, so helping your plants to put down deep roots, establish well and grow strongly.

Digging also allows you to add compost and well-rotted manure. As well as increasing soil fertility, humus-rich materials both improve drainage and assist in water retention, so are extremely useful on all types of soil, from sandy to clay. They also support worms and other earth-dwellers, which can then play their role in keeping the soil healthy. Digging to a spade's depth should be sufficient on most reasonable soil. Where the soil has never been cultivated, is full of rubbish or is poorly drained, double digging is a great way to improve its overall health. Double digging gets down into lower layers, loosens any

HOW TO dig and improve your soil

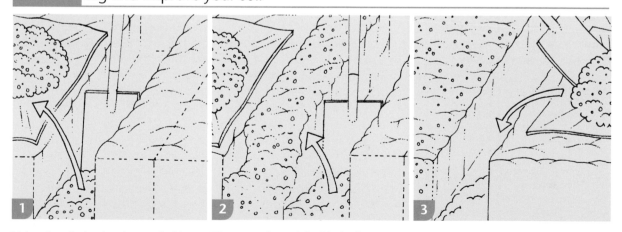

1 Make a trench about as deep and wide as a spade's blade. Set aside the soil you've dug on plastic sheeting. (To double dig, fork over the trench base and push the tines to their full depth to aerate the soil.)

2 Dig a second trench beside the first, and turn the soil from the second trench into the first one. Add as much organic matter as you can as you go. Continue in this way until you get to the final trench.

3 Fill the final trench, which will now be empty, with the soil on the sheeting that was taken from the first trench; add organic matter. Go over the whole area and break up any lumps with a fork.

compaction and increases fertility and aeration, all beneficial for the future occupants. This is especially useful in vegetable plots, where plants have to grow fast and be highly productive, and where flooding has occurred (*see* page 18).

There is a school of thought that says 'no dig' is best, instead adding organic matter as a mulch and leaving the work to nature, but even gardeners who shun the ritual annual digging of a veg garden usually dig their plot once at the very beginning. It's always helpful to remove large stones and weeds, and you also learn a lot about your soil through digging it.

Planting

Whatever you are planting, plant it properly. Poorly planted specimens are less likely to establish well and may even die. With pot-grown plants, dig a hole twice as deep as the existing rootball and four times as wide, to give the plant a tempting area of loose soil to send its roots out into. Dry potting compost tends to resist water, so water the plant well about an hour or so before you

Don't forget

Mycorrhizal fungi in the soil help plants to establish. To increase their effect, add mycorrhizal fungal granules when you plant.

Give them space

Diseases such as downy mildew and botrytis are more likely to occur where air circulation is poor, so make sure you leave plenty of space around your plants. This is particularly important with annual bedding plants, which don't have much time to put down roots and establish well before they have to begin flowering.

HOW TO plant a shrub

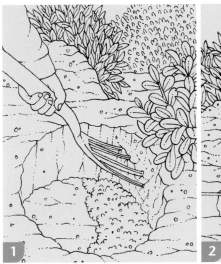

1 Dig a hole at least four times the width and twice the depth of the rootball. Loosen the soil around the sides and base to make it easier for roots to penetrate. Mix compost and slow-release fertilizer into the soil removed from the hole.

2 Put some of the enriched excavated soil back into the hole, adjusting until the top of the plant's rootball is level with the top of the hole. Tease out the plant roots a little. Backfill, easing soil around the plant, firm it in well and water thoroughly.

intend to plant it otherwise it might die of thirst, even if you water it copiously after planting.

Slide the plant out of its pot and gently tease out the roots if necessary. This is particularly important if the roots are very matted, because they will tend to stay within the existing rootball and never venture out into the soil. It is horribly disheartening to dig up a plant that has failed to thrive and find it has grown a bunch of tightly packed roots that would all fit back into the original pot.

For trees, shrubs and perennials, mix some slow-release fertilizer (*see* page 24) and humus-rich material into the soil that you have dug out. Return some of the soil into the bottom of the hole and place the

plant centrally. Make sure the soil level around the plant is the same as the soil level in the pot. Planting too deeply may cause the stems to rot, while planting too shallowly exposes the roots and potting compost, leading to drying out and the risk of wind rock. Backfill around the roots and firm the soil surface so the plant is snugly planted. Water well and then spread a layer of mulch, 5cm (2in) thick, of compost or chipped bark around the plant to seal in moisture and reduce competition from weeds. Trees and some shrubs will need staking. Staking prevents the top of the plant moving too much in the wind and enables the plant to grow finer roots, which it needs to take up water and nutrients.

Pruning and trimming

Although many plants never need the touch of secateurs or shears, there are times when a trim is the difference between life and death. Diseases can enter through a rub or split in bark and quickly spread once inside the plant. Inspect trees and shrubs regularly and remove growth that is weak, dead or dying, rubbing, too long, or growing the wrong way. Trimming herbaceous plants once their growth has died back in autumn leaves no home for pests and diseases and gives the new growth a clear run in spring.

Long-handled loppers are ideal for tackling overgrown shrubs, such as this weigela. Be decisive and make neat cuts at a slight angle.

Watering

Water is top of the list of plant requirements. Lack of water is among the most common causes of plant death, although too much water is also a killer (*see* page 18).

The first job after planting is watering. Give all plants a good soak: trees and shrubs need at least a watering-canful. This settles the roots into the soil as well as giving them a drink. Unless they are planted in the autumn, most plants need regular watering*– once or twice a week – until they have put out new roots and are growing strongly. Make sure you give plenty each time. A little sprinkle does more harm than good, since it encourages the roots to hang around at the surface rather than going down deeply into the soil.

Dry plants are much more susceptible to diseases such as powdery mildew and pests like red spider mite, and they won't grow, flower or crop well, so it is certainly worth watering even established plants during dry spells. Vegetables, container plants and those in greenhouses need much more water than those in the open garden, so if you don't have much time concentrate on these.

If you have perfect soil, you need not worry too much about over-watering or drought, but most of us need to take a little more care. Both cause similar symptoms: foliage wilts, roots disintegrate, plants die back or die altogether. With drought or erratic watering, flowers and fruit may also not form, fruit may split or drop, and crops run to seed early.

Gardener's damage

Take care not to damage your plants by accident. Something as simple as water splashed on leaves in strong sun can concentrate rays like a mini-magnifying glass, causing scorched spots that dry out and die.

If you use weedkiller to fight back against weeds (*see* page 34), remember that any drift or splash onto nearby plants can cause foliage to grow twisted and narrow or turn yellow, even if it doesn't kill the plant. If you use a strimmer, take particular care around the base of trees, or you may cut through their bark and weaken or kill them.

When pruning, use sharp tools: untidy cuts can cause dieback and are unsightly. Remove large branches in stages to avoid tearing the bark, and never cut closer than the outer edge of the swollen 'collar' where they join the trunk.

Don't forget

If you are pruning in winter and not sure whether a branch is dead, scratch a little of the bark with a fingernail. Green underneath indicates it is still alive.

Digging up

Plants can become sickly because they are growing in the wrong conditions, are being crowded by their neighbours or have just outgrown their space. Even quite large shrubs and young trees can be transplanted with care, and often it is worth trying anyway, because the alternative is death.

Moving is best done in the autumn, though any time until late winter is acceptable. If possible, begin by pruning back the top-growth by up to one third; this will compensate for the loss of roots. Dig all around the plant to the depth of a spade, inserting the blade vertically into the soil. Undercut the plant at this depth, severing the remaining roots until you have freed it from the soil. Prepare the new planting hole and then transfer the plant to its new home, taking care to avoid disturbing the remaining roots as far as possible. Water and stake as necessary.

Rejuvenation

After a few years of healthy growth and wonderful blooms, spreading perennials such as irises, hardy geraniums, crocosmias and daylilies (*Hemerocallis*) start to die out in the middle of the clump or become very overcrowded. They produce fewer flowers and generally make much less of a contribution to the garden. Many bulbs behave in a similar way, growing masses of grassy leaves and producing no blooms. Fortunately, the remedy is straightforward: they need to be dug up, split into smaller clumps – keep the youngest and healthiest bits – and then replanted

HOW TO move an established shrub

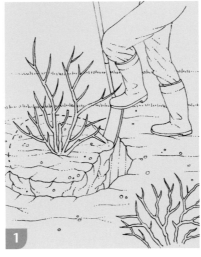

1

Cut straight down into the ground all around the shrub, just outside the extent of its branches.

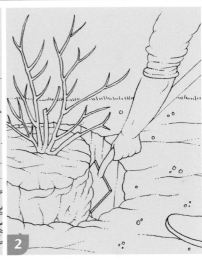

2

Undercut the rootball at an angle of 45 degrees. You will need to cut through some roots.

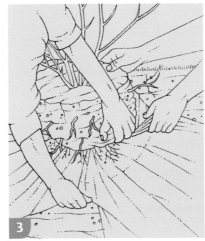

3

With help if possible, ease a sheet of thick polythene or sacking under the rootball. It is easiest to do this by rocking the plant to one side and then the other.

4

Use the sheet to carry the shrub to its new home. Replant it carefully (*see* page 21) and water it well until it is re-established and growing away.

in soil that has been refreshed with plenty of humus-rich material. Well-organized gardeners will lift and divide their plants before they

reach the really tired stage, thereby avoiding the risk of disease and pest invasion as well as keeping their garden looking good.

Feeding

If they are planted in well-prepared ground that contains plenty of humus-rich material, trees, shrubs and hedging plants usually do very well without additional food, as do the great majority of herbaceous perennials. However, there are some plants that flower better if they are given a regular top-up. Many vegetables, especially fruiting types such as tomatoes, must also be fed in order to remain healthy and crop well. Make a point of getting to know the food requirements of all the plants in your care.

Acid-loving plants, such as camellias and rhododendrons, benefit from a feed of ericaceous fertilizer in spring. Sprinkle the granules lightly on the soil surface around the plant. This will prevent chlorosis (yellowing of the leaves).

Slow food

In gardens with a thin or light soil, such as those that contain a high proportion of sand or peat (*see* page 14), an annual top-dressing of a slow-release fertilizer can be very beneficial. As their name implies, slow-release fertilizers put nutrients into the soil over a long period of time. They come as powders, pellets or granules and are simply sprinkled over the ground. They can also be scattered in and around the planting hole when planting. There are both organic and inorganic varieties. The organic ones are based on animal by-products, such as chicken manure or hoof and horn. Seaweed meal is also available. The inorganic varieties are synthesized chemicals or extracted minerals.

Slow-release fertilizers, particularly the inorganic ones, are often balanced, or general-purpose. They contain similar quantities of the main plant nutrients – nitrogen (N), phosphate (P) and potassium or potash (K) – and can be used as an all-round feed. However, many of the organic varieties are rich in one nutrient rather than having the same amount of all three. This means they are particularly useful if you want to feed for specific results, such as high fruit yields or lush leaves. They are also handy if you suspect your garden soil is deficient in certain nutrients (*see* opposite).

Hungry plants

The most hungry of all plants are fruit and vegetables, which are expected to produce large amounts of growth and often fruit crops in a comparatively short space of time. But some ornamentals, such as clematis and roses, as well as all plants in pots, will also perform better for regular feeding. Liquid or water-soluble fertilizers, which can be delivered to the roots or used as a foliar feed, are a good way of getting food into the plant quickly and can be used up to once a week. These feeds are either general-purpose or formulated for specific uses. Tomato feed is one of the best-known specific feeds and contains nutrients needed for fruit production. There are also specific products available for particular deficiencies: for example, ericaceous feeds are aimed at acid-loving plants, such as rhododendrons and camellias. Plants that are suffering from deficiencies can be given these feeds as a tonic when needed.

Be wary of overfeeding

Before feeding, always check what your plants need. It is possible to overfeed, and the results can be lush foliage growth at the expense of flowers and fruit, and poor-flavoured or even inedible fruit (*see* Apple bitter pit, page 100). Crops like carrots and beetroot can develop 'fanged' or divided roots if overfed (*see* page 110). Herbs prefer to be on poor soil with low nutrient levels, while annuals are best planted into well-prepared beds and not given additional feed except on very poor soils.

Don't forget

Don't feed plants that are in dry soil. They won't be able to benefit from the feed, and their roots may be scorched.

Nutrient deficiencies are relatively rare in most gardens, especially those where the plants have been properly planted and are subsequently well tended. However, they can occur, particularly on sandy, chalky and other light soils, where nutrients may be washed out by rain. Inexpensive kits to test for soil nutrients are available at garden centres and are simple to use. Nutrient problems may also be found where plants are growing in conditions that just don't suit them. For example, acid-loving plants on alkaline soil are unable to take up the nutrients they need. There are feeds specially formulated to remedy most deficiencies.

Because they are the main sites of food production, leaves are also usually the first part of a plant to show nutrient deficiencies.

① Low nitrogen levels in the soil can show up as yellow or even pink colouring in the leaves.

② Scorched brown leaf edges and purple or yellow coloration are often a sign that the plant is not getting enough potassium.

③ Lack of magnesium makes the leaves become yellow between the leaf veins; the foliage may develop red or brown patches.

Main nutrients

■ **Nitrogen** (N) is needed for leaf production and it is the most common deficiency. A lack of nitrogen results in poor growth; the plant's leaves are pale green and may turn yellow or even pinkish. Nitrogen deficiency is particularly likely in potted plants, because their roots are restricted and unable to seek out their own nutrients. It may also be caused by lack of light in crowded or heavily shaded plants that cannot photosynthesize effectively. In gardens it is found in light soils after periods of heavy rain.

■ **Phosphorus** (P), one of the main plant nutrients, is needed for strong roots, but shortages are rare in gardens. Where they occur the leaves become dull yellow and growth is slow.

■ **Potassium** (potash, K) is needed for strong roots and deficiencies are most common on light soils. The leaves become tinted with yellow or purple, and their edges start to turn brown.

The problem of greenback in tomatoes can be a result of potassium deficiency, as can whitish flesh (*see* Tomato problems, pages 106–8).

Micronutrients

■ **Boron** is a rare deficiency, but this micronutrient can be short where plants are growing in alkaline conditions. A lack of boron causes heart rot in beetroot, brown heart in turnips and swedes and brown curds in cauliflowers (*see* page 101).

■ **Calcium** shortage may occur in apples, tomatoes and peppers. It causes bitter pit in apples (*see* page 100), and blossom end rot in tomatoes (*see* page 106) and peppers. Dry soil can prevent plants taking up the calcium they need.

■ **Magnesium** deficiency – again common on light soils – is most frequently seen in chrysanthemums, raspberries, rhododendrons, roses, apples, grapes and tomatoes. Initially,

the leaves discolour to yellow; they may develop red or brown blotches and fall early. Overfeeding can cause magnesium deficiencies, because plants take up the potassium in feeds in preference to the magnesium.

■ **Manganese** is a rare deficiency, but it can occur in acid-loving plants growing in alkaline soil or in normal potting composts (ericaceous potting compost is specially formulated for acid-loving plants). Its symptoms are similar to magnesium deficiency: yellowing between the leaf veins and browning of leaf edges. Speckled yellows in beetroots is due to manganese deficiency: yellow patches appear between the leaf veins and eventually the leaf rolls up. Spinach suffers in a similar way.

■ **Molybdenum** shortage is mostly found in brassicas on acid soil. It causes a condition called whiptail (*see* page 92), in which the leaves are elongated, twisted and very narrow.

Dealing with problems

Sometimes, despite the best care and attention, plants become sickly or fall prey to pests. When you do spot a problem, it is advisable to diagnose it sooner rather than later, and in many cases early treatment is most effective. However, often no action is necessary and in some cases there is nothing that you can do. (For individual ailments and how to treat them, *see* Plant problems and remedies, pages 60–113.)

Copper is thought to give slugs and snails a small electric shock, which puts them off touching it, so these rings should protect the pea plants growing inside them.

Pests

The majority of insect pests cause disfigurement but are not fatal. Small infestations on low-growing plants can be removed by hand. For example, aphids often cluster around shoot-tips and flower buds, and it is fairly easy to rub them off gently or give them a squirt with a hosepipe. Preventative measures can be effective in other cases – carrot fly, narcissus bulb fly, slugs and snails and mammals can be controlled using barriers. Deterrents, such as companion plants (*see* page 11), can also be successful.

However, you need a different approach for major attacks by very damaging insects such as sawflies, which can't be picked off, or by microscopic pests, such as red spider mites. Some can be combated with biological controls (*see* opposite), or you may feel that an insecticide is justified, but these are not a cure-all.

Diseases

Choosing healthy plants and looking after them well reduces diseases in your garden. Ailments may still occur, and for many there is no cure, but few are fatal except to young plants. Fungal infections are among the most common, causing cankers and diebacks, rusts, smuts, mildews, wilts and leaf spotting, all of which are unattractive and undesirable. With woody plants, judicious pruning is the best way to keep such diseases to a minimum. Localized infections can be controlled by removing the affected parts; for widespread problems you may need to resort to a fungicide. Mildews and wilts are generally the result of poor growing conditions.

Fungal or bacterial rots usually appear in damp conditions, and are damaging to plants and produce. They can be avoided only by better cultivation and storage practices.

Viruses may be imported on new, seemingly fit plants, or come in via insects such as aphids. Fortunately, only a few plants are susceptible, but there are no treatments and all the affected plants are best destroyed.

Don't forget

Diagnosing plant problems can be tricky, but there is only a handful of treatments for pests and diseases, so choosing one is not a very complicated business.

Types of pesticides

As a rule, organic pesticides (*see* opposite) are based on natural ingredients, whereas non-organic versions are laboratory formulations. Some products combine the two.

All pesticides sold for amateurs have been carefully tested under strict conditions and must have a licence before they can be sold. The licence can be revoked or amended, and this is not always because of anything harmful in the product; sometimes it is because the manufacturer wants to modify it in some way. Non-organic products are subject to change, although most contain similar combinations of ingredients. The label will tell you what problem the product is currently licensed to treat.

For more information about chemicals, *see* www.pesticides.gov.uk. This website also tells you when a product has been or is about to be banned, so is useful if you have old bottles lurking in the shed.

Indiscriminate use of any pesticide – organic or non-organic – is inadvisable because all affect beneficial insects too. Make sure that the pesticide you choose is suitable for the plant you want to treat and follow the instructions to the letter. On edible plants, check the time between application and harvest.

Organic pesticides

Organic pesticides tend to be 'contact' products, which kill only on contact, whereas systemic ones are also partially absorbed into the plant and so continue to work for up to four weeks. This means you have to be prepared to apply organic pesticides at the right time to catch the target and reapply them as necessary. Pesticides and fungicides are sometimes combined in one product.

PROBLEM	REMEDY	NOTES
Blight, fungal and bacterial infections	Bordeaux mixture	Preventative spray of copper sulphate and calcium hydroxide. Persistent and toxic.
Mildews, black spot	Potassium bicarbonate	Contact killer, sometimes combined with soaps or oils for adhesion.
Fungal infections or insects	Sulphur	Contact killer dust, or spray with fatty acids (*see* Soft soap, below). Can damage some plants; try on a small area first.
	Soft soap or insecticidal soap	Contact killer spray containing potassium salts of fatty acids in alcohol. Toxic to aquatic life. Its safety is under scrutiny.
	Sesame oil/fish oil blend	Used as a spray, this smothers rather than poisons insects, making it safe around water, and provides some fungal protection.
Insects	Grease or glue bands	For monitoring winter moth activity; usually made from rapeseed oil.
	Pheromone traps	For monitoring moth activity; different sorts detect different species.
	Plant oils	Contact killer sprays based on rapeseed oils; supposedly safe around ladybirds, bees and lacewings.
	Pyrethrum	Contact killer with extracts of *Pyrethrum cinerariifolium*. Very toxic to aquatic life; also kills bees.
	Sticky traps	Hung in greenhouses to trap flying insects.
	Winter tree wash	Plant oil spray, kills overwintering insect eggs by suffocating them.
Slugs	Ferric phosphate pellets	Safe around children, pets and wildlife.

Biological controls

Biological controls are products that make use of naturally occurring organisms to combat pests. Every garden pest has a predator and some of these can be bred and packaged for timed release to reduce pest numbers where they have become a problem. Biological controls are usually insect larvae or nematodes (eelworms) that live on or in the pest, eventually killing it. Biological controls work best in the greenhouse. Of those listed, only the ones for ants, caterpillars, chafer grubs, leatherjackets and slugs are suitable for outdoor use.

PEST	BIOLOGICAL CONTROL	HOW TO USE
Ant and leatherjacket	*Steinernema feltiae* (pathogenic nematode)	Mix powder with water and water into nests. Soil must be at 10–12°C (50–54°F). Powder has short use-by period.
Aphid	*Aphidius* species (parastic wasp larva)	Release near aphids. Most effective under cover at over 15°C (60°F).
Caterpillar	*Steinernema carpocapsae* (pathogenic nematode)	Mix powder with water and spray affected plants. Difficult to treat large trees. Needs repeat applications.
Chafer grub	*Heterorhabditis megidis* (pathogenic nematode)	Mix powder with water and apply to lawn. Needs damp conditions. Use at 12°C (54°F) or above.
Mealy bug	*Cryptolaemus montrouzieri* (pathogenic nematode)	Release near mealy bugs. Must be used under cover and needs warmth and light to work.
Red spider mite	*Phytoseiulus persimilis* (predatory mite)	Release on infested plants. Works best at 18–22°C (64–72°F), so only suitable under cover. May need a second treatment.
Scale insect	*Metaphycus helvolus* (parasitic wasp) *Encyrtus infelix* (parasitic mite)	Release them on the infested plants. Work best at 20–30°C (68–86°F), so suitable only under cover.
Slug	*Phasmarhabditis hermaphrodita* (pathogenic nematode)	Mix powder with water and apply to soil. Works for six weeks only. Must be used in moist conditions at 5°C (40°F).
Vine weevil larva	*Steinernema kraussei* (pathogenic nematode)	Mix powder with water and apply to soil at least twice a year at 5°C (40°F) or above.
Whitefly	*Encarsia formosa* (parastic wasp)	Hang cards containing the wasp around infested plants. Needs 12 or more daylight hours and temperatures above 21°C (70°F).

Garden weeds

Weeds are plants we don't want in our gardens. This can include some ornamentals that make themselves too much at home and threaten to take over, but mostly means plants that are unattractive in one way or another. Because they are usually native plants and perfectly adapted to local conditions, weeds easily outperform our carefully tended ornamentals. They are not completely resistant to pests or diseases, but are so tough that they shrug them off, while giving them a springboard from which to leap onto our precious crops or decorative plants. Or that's the way it can seem.

Introducing weeds

Weeds come in as many shapes and sizes as any other plant found in gardens. They can be annuals, perennials, climbers, shrubs and trees. They can even have pretty flowers or attractive leaves. Some of our much-loved garden plants are weeds – or as good as – in their countries of origin. Conversely, some plants imported into our gardens from abroad because they were considered decorative have gone on to prove themselves less than pleasant in other ways.

What makes a weed?

The main thing that makes a plant a weed is its ability to reproduce at speed. Anything that increases a gardener's workload in this way is bound to be regarded as a pest. Weeds are usually good at self-seeding: they produce masses of seed and every single one seems to germinate. Dandelions, thistles and ash trees are good examples. Even the rather lovely red campion can become a nuisance due to the sheer number of seeds contained within its pretty, pitcher-shaped capsules.

The second thing that makes a plant a weed is that it is hard to control and quickly spreads where it is not wanted. Even when the gardener makes a concerted effort to get rid of it, it manages to regrow, reappear and generally make a nuisance of itself. Weeds seem to sprout at twice the speed

The seedhead of the dandelion is soft and beautiful if you look at it without prejudice. But when it reaches this stage, a single puff of wind will scatter these little seed-laden parachutes far and wide across the garden.

Bindweed does what its name implies to anything and everything in the garden, slowly choking plants such as this lysimachia. Although it is easy to prevent from seeding, its deep roots make it hard to eradicate.

of other plants, and they often go on growing until late into the autumn and start early in spring. Lesser celandine is an early starter, while hairy bittercress simply never stops. Many of them have roots that can grow new plants from the tiniest fragment. This includes bindweed, ground elder and couch grass, all of which relish being chopped into bits by an overzealous gardener with a spade – it won't stop them.

Finally, weeds often just don't look right. Their tendency to spread means they make too much of an impact. Even those that are attractive insist on appearing in the wrong place, spoiling carefully considered designs. The flowers of bindweed, for example, are beautiful trumpets of white or pink, yet it is not content with shinning up one plant and displaying itself elegantly. It has to take over whole sections of garden, smothering all in its path. But the truth is that many weeds are simply not pretty enough to be given any garden room.

Don't forget

Weeds are not all bad. Their flowers provide nectar for many beneficial insects and the leaves can make excellent food for the caterpillars of our native butterflies.

Weeding equipment

Gardeners spend a lot of time weeding, so it's worth investing in some tools specifically designed for that task. Most gardeners find one or two that they use nearly all the time, occasionally resorting to something else when the need arises. The items described here all have their place in the tool shed.

Choosing tools

For any sort of gardening, a good-quality spade and border fork are invaluable. They do the major soil-moving jobs, as well as the planting work. However, except in vegetable gardens, they are less useful for weeding once the initial preparation is over. For routine weeding, slightly more slender tools are required to ferret around among your plants and root out the interlopers. Most of them are small hand tools.

Hand fork This can be used vertically to dig out well-rooted weeds, such as brambles and buttercup, and with the tines at 45 degrees or less to tousle the soil's surface, uprooting or beheading softer weeds. Choose one with a comfortable handle.

Dandelion grubber There are two sorts of grubber: one resembles a two-tined fork with wide, flat tines and a single, long slit between them, and the other has a small, V-shaped 'blade' at the end of a longish shaft. They are used to get down through the soil to the depths reached by dandelions and other tap-rooters such as plantain, dock and thistles. You can bring out most of the root, but rarely the whole thing.

Patio knife A narrow implement with an L-shaped blade, this is used between paving slabs and along other cracks with the intention of uprooting weeds and removing other debris. An old kitchen knife will do a similar job, if it has a good strong blade, but is less efficient at hoicking out roots.

Flame-gun Flame-guns are used to burn off the top-growth of weeds and are useful where digging out is not an option. They are useful on areas of bare ground or on paths and patios. However, they don't kill the roots, so repeat visits will be necessary. Also, the heat they generate is harmful to soil organisms, so use them carefully.

Kneeler and gloves These two items make a gardener's life a little more comfortable. The kneeler can be sat on as well as knelt upon. Kneeling pads are fastened around your knees to protect them from bruising and your trousers from being worn out. They are a popular alternative to a kneeler and more suitable for when you are moving among plants. Rubberized gloves protect your hands, provide a reasonable grip and still allow a certain amount of 'feel'. They are useful for pulling up a range of weeds, including stinging nettles and thistles.

Hoes There are three main hoe types: Dutch (or push) hoe, draw (or chop) hoe and hand (or onion) hoe. Dutch hoes have a slightly angled blade at the end of a long handle. They are designed for pushing forwards through the top layer of soil, uprooting or beheading weeds as they go. The blade of a draw hoe is fixed at more of an angle to the handle. It is used drawn backwards in a chopping motion to separate weed leaves from weed roots. The hand hoe is a smaller version of a draw hoe, suitable for use among more delicate plants and seedlings.

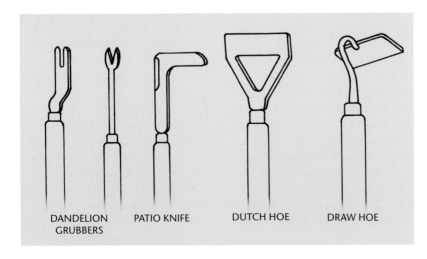

DANDELION GRUBBERS   PATIO KNIFE   DUTCH HOE   DRAW HOE

Weed prevention and control

There is a well-known saying in gardening circles: one year's weeds make seven years' seeds. While it is true that you don't want to allow weeds to set seed, it is also a fact that weeds have been dropping their seeds in gardens for centuries and you can never be rid of them all. The best you can hope to achieve is reasonable control. There are four main ways to achieve this: good soil preparation, routine weeding, physical barriers and, as a last resort, weedkillers.

Soil preparation

In a new border or in the vegetable garden the first step to weed control is good soil preparation. Double digging (*see* page 20) will help you to remove the worst of the perennial weed roots. If there are areas of ground elder, bindweed, couch grass or any other weeds that can regrow from pieces of root (*see* page 32), take care to remove as much as possible, very carefully. This is comparatively easy on reasonably dry, well-dug soil, as the roots can often be eased out gently in long strands. They are mostly simple to spot too, often being white and widespreading. On compacted soils it will take several goes. Don't try to do it all at once. With new borders, dig and remove weeds, then allow a few weeks for them to regrow, before gently working through the soil again. You still won't get rid of everything, but you'll have removed the worst of them. Vegetable beds

One of the most satisfying jobs in the garden is clearing and digging over beds and borders to eradicate weeds. It's good, warming exercise too.

get worked over so often that in the course of a few years most weeds will reduce greatly in numbers.

Every time you dig soil you bring annual weed seeds to the surface, where they germinate. They will appear in large quantities after you have made a new border or vegetable bed or gone over an old one thoroughly, particularly if you have added compost or manure, as both these will also almost inevitably introduce weed seeds. A few weeks after doing the second lot of digging for perennial weed roots, go over the soil surface to remove weeds that have germinated, using a hoe, a hand fork, your fingers or a flame-gun. Avoid disturbing the soil too much, since this will bring more seeds to the surface.

Untouched ground

Where the soil has never been cultivated, or is overrun with a wide range of weeds, it is often easiest to resort to a herbicide containing glyphosate. This will need at least two applications to kill off the worst of the weeds, but will take a lot of the slog out of the soil preparation.

Many gardeners with organic leanings are prepared to use glyphosate as a one-off at the start before returning to a no-chemical regime. Glyphosate is not persistent in the soil and is widely regarded as relatively harmless, but it is toxic to aquatic life and should be used carefully and strictly according to the instructions on the packet. Remember that it will kill all plants, not only weeds (*see* page 34).

Routine weeding

Once you have plants growing in your flower beds or vegetable patch, it's a good idea to weed on a fairly regular basis. If you do it often, you keep on top of the problem and it can be quick and relatively painless. The weeds don't get a chance to root deeply, establish or set seed, making them easier to strip out from between your prized specimens and less likely to have made their presence too obvious. If, as you weed, you come across any of those perennial types with re-shooting roots, you have three options: make further efforts to ease the whole root out, remove all the top-growth, or use a spot herbicide (*see* page 34). With any of these, it is unlikely that you will get rid of the weed entirely at the first attempt, but if you are conscientious and revisit the spot every week to remove any regrowth, even the most persistent troublemaker will eventually give up.

Physical barriers

Once you have got on top of the worst of the weeds – usually through a lot of hard work – consider the options for keeping them away. Two of the best are weedproof membranes and mulches.

Weedproof membranes

Sometimes called landscaping fabrics, geotextiles, or even sheet mulches, these are lightweight, dark-coloured fabrics made from strong, UV-stabilized material, usually either spun or woven polypropylene. There are various weights of both varieties, and all allow water through but reduce or block light levels at the soil surface so prevent weed germination and growth. Spun types are softer, lighter and cheaper than woven, but won't last as long.

These materials have several major uses in the garden. They are excellent as ground cover where you

Warning: don't compost!

Most weeds can be composted, unless they're in seed or you've used weedkiller. Don't risk composting the following:

Bindweed (p.35)	Horsetail (p.37)
Couch grass (p.37)	Japanese knotweed (p.38)
Creeping thistle (p.36)	Knotgrass (p.54)
Dandelion (p.41)	Lesser celandine (p.39)
Broad-leaved dock (p.40)	Speedwell (p.41)
Ground elder (p.35)	Winter heliotrope (p.38)

Careful hoeing between vegetables ensures the weeds never take over and prevents soil from forming a crust that water cannot penetrate. The mats in the foreground help protect strawberry plants, which have shallow roots, easily damaged by hoeing.

are planning to have a bed or border of permanent plants, particularly shrubs and trees. Lay the membrane over the prepared soil and then make holes in it and plant through them. It will suppress weeds while the plants establish.

As an alternative to using weedkiller, membranes can be laid over weedy areas that are intended for cultivation. The lack of light will kill off the weeds' top-growth, making the job of digging much easier. They are also useful for covering fallow vegetable patches. For example, if you dig and manure a bed in the autumn, covering it with fabric over winter will prevent weeds sprouting and will help the soil to warm up earlier in spring in preparation for planting. Spreading plants, such as melons and squashes, can be trained over landscaping fabrics, reducing the need for weeding and at the same time keeping the developing fruit clean.

Finally, the tougher, woven fabrics are a good base for paths and other walkways. Apart from in the vegetable garden, they are best covered with gravel chippings or bark (*see* Mulches, below) since they are not very attractive. These toppings will eventually produce a hoard of weed seedlings themselves, but the fabric beneath prevents them from rooting deeply, so they are easily removed.

Mulches

As well as disguising weedproof membranes, mulches can be used alone to reduce weed growth, while also slowing water evaporation from the soil. In addition, organic mulches such as bark, leaf mould and compost act as long-term soil conditioners, providing low levels of nutrients as they rot down. Garden centres sell a range of suitable products, which should be weed-free. Home-made compost isn't ideal because it often contains weed seeds.

Gravel comes in a wide range of colours, shapes and sizes and is useful as a permanent mulch on paths and patios as well as for scree or riverbed-style gardens. It is more expensive than organic mulches but lasts much longer and produces a more sophisticated effect.

Path and patio weeds

Because they are tough and can live anywhere, weeds soon take up residence between paving stones and cracks in concrete. Here, they often need fairly swift attention. For a start, they are usually much more obvious and unsightly than they are among other plants in flower beds and borders. Second, they can root very deeply, which soon makes them difficult to get out, as well as eventually undermining the paving. Patio knives and other thin tools, such as old kitchen knives, can winkle out most young weeds. Where there are many small weeds

A narrow blade, such as this old bone-handled knife, is just what's needed to dislodge persistent weeds from crevices between path or patio flagstones.

Compost makes an excellent mulch that will discourage weeds (unless it contains their seeds), retain water and condition the soil. At the same time, it has the benefit of instantly making everything look neat and well tended.

Wear protective gloves and goggles when using a flame-gun. Do the job slowly and always direct the flame downwards.

This persistence means they are more likely to be environmentally damaging. Sprays are best for spot killing of one or two weeds, while for larger areas concentrates are a better bet. With concentrates, use a watering can or other container and clearly mark it to ensure you don't use it for any other purpose, because the slightest trace left in it can damage your prized plants.

There are relatively few organic weedkillers. Those that are available tend to be based on fatty acids or acetic acid (vinegar) and are sometimes intended to kill only moss and algae on hard surfaces.

Over the last few years, the number of weedkilling chemicals available to gardeners has reduced markedly, just as with pesticides (*see* page 26), and the chemicals used in products are similarly subject to change. However, glyphosate is a common ingredient in a number of products and it is the chemical most widely recommended for general use on flower beds or in vegetable plots, because it has systemic action, which means it kills the plant roots as well as the top-growth. As soon as it touches the soil, glyphosate is deactivated and broken down by bacteria, which is why it is thought not to be too harmful to the environment. However, it is combined with other chemicals in some formulations, which can be more persistent or toxic.

that would take an age to pull out by hand, a flame-gun comes in handy. These are comparatively inexpensive and make quick work of burning off the top-growth. However, they do not kill roots, so you may need to revisit the same spot a few times. Be particularly careful if using them near wooden structures and anything plastic.

Using weedkillers

Where a problem is widespread, you might want to use a herbicide, or weedkiller. However, because of concerns over chemicals and their effects on the environment, it makes

sense, wherever possible, to try non-chemical methods first.

Many weedkillers are non-selective, which means that they kill all plants, not only the ones you are targeting. Most of those available to amateur gardeners are also non-residual, which means they do not persist in the soil for any length of time – this is a good thing, because it limits their environmental impact. However, weedkillers that are formulated for use on paths and patios can be persistent – that is, have a long-lasting action – as the manufacturers reason that you don't want to be using them frequently.

Don't forget

Weedkillers should not be used near water as they're toxic to aquatic life; also, keep them out of reach of children and pets. Do not put plants killed by weedkillers on the compost heap.

Gallery of garden weeds

As with ornamental plants, some weeds thrive in certain parts of the country, yet the same species may hardly be noticed elsewhere. Many weeds can be tolerated in low numbers or are easy to remove, while it takes concerted effort to control or eradicate others. For your own peace of mind, accept that your garden will never be weed-free and concentrate on just keeping the worst in check. The weeds shown in this gallery are perennial unless otherwise stated.

Bindweed
Calystegia sepium, Convolvulus arvensis
If they didn't spread so easily, bindweeds would make beautiful climbing plants. *Convolvulus* (above) has white flowers often marked with pink, while those of *Calystegia* are usually plain white. Both have slender stems that run along the ground or twine around plants and other supports. Their thick, white roots go very deep but also run horizontally, growing stems and leaves wherever they surface.

With small patches, remove top-growth weekly to weaken and eventually kill the plants or use a spot weedkiller; larger areas may need several treatments with glyphosate. Digging out requires great care, since the roots break easily, each piece producing a new plant.

Ground elder
Aegiopodium podagraria
This pungent weed spreads swiftly by underground runners. It soon invades a well-dug border, getting among plants where control is very difficult. Where it is established, the solution is to dig up ornamentals and extricate the runners from their roots, remove as much as possible from the soil, then allow time for any remaining bits to regrow and treat them with glyphosate. Don't replant until you are sure all the elder is gone. With smaller patches, repeatedly remove the top-growth or use a spot weedkiller.

Shepherd's purse
Capsella bursa-pastoris
This rather romantically named annual has low rosettes of leaves, from the middle of which the tall flower stems can appear almost all the year round. The heart-shaped seed capsule is the 'purse'. The plants are easily pulled out by hand or removed using a hand fork or hoe. Do not put plants on the compost heap if seedheads have already formed, because the seed will continue to mature. Glyphosate is an option on large areas, but not really necessary.

Hairy bittercress
Cardamine hirsuta
This small annual weed germinates year-round and rapidly reaches flowering size. It grows in a range of conditions including under plant leaves. The shallow-rooted plants are easily removed by hand or using a hand fork or hoe. Do this before they set seed, since disturbing them once the seed is ripe can set off the catapult-like seeding mechanism, spreading them far and wide across the garden. Seedheads continue to mature after digging up, so be wary of putting the plants on the compost heap.

Creeping thistle
Cirsium arvense
This spreads by underground stems as well as seed, and it likes well-cultivated, moist soil. The roots may grow several metres deep. They break easily and pieces are capable of producing new plants; they may remain dormant in the soil for many years, resprouting when digging brings them to the surface. Hoeing off the top-growth is unlikely to succeed; well-established roots quickly produce new leaf buds and take a long time to give up. Use spot weedkiller for individuals, or treat larger areas with glyphosate. In lawns, regular mowing will eventually kill them.

Couch grass
Elytrigia repens
Couch often starts off in a lawn, where the mower keeps it under control. However, when it reaches flower beds, it quickly spreads under plants and proves very persistent. Its roots are as tough as wire, until you come to pull them up – then they snap easily, each piece forming a new plant. Maintain a clear edge between lawn and flower beds to prevent it wandering. If careful digging is unsuccessful, try a spot weedkiller. Use a weedproof membrane (*see* pages 32–3) or glyphosate on large patches.

Horsetail
Equisetum arvense
Along with Japanese knotweed (*see* page 38), this spreading, deep-rooting plant really deserves the epithet 'pernicious'. It is almost impossible to eradicate, since weedkillers of all kinds have little long-term effect on it. If you resort to weedkillers, bruise the stems first, because their waxy surface acts as a repellent. If you are a very energetic gardener and the weed is on open ground, such as a vegetable patch, regular hoeing will eventually weaken it. Tough, weedproof membranes may reduce its spread and keep it out of immediate sight.

Sun spurge
Euphorbia helioscopia
This little annual has bright green leaves topped with yellowish-green flowers. When ripe, the copious seeds are ejected fairly long distances, so it is important not to let it set seed. The seedlings are fairly easy to pull by hand or using a hand fork, or they can be hoed off. Larger plants tend to break up when pulled, making the task a little more arduous. Wear gloves to keep the irritating sap from getting onto your skin. Chemical controls should not be necessary.

Japanese knotweed
Fallopia japonica

One of the best-known pernicious weeds and almost impossible to control, this was introduced as a garden plant in the 19th century and has been making a nuisance of itself ever since. Shoots can pierce through concrete and tarmac, and new plants grow from the tiniest pieces of root. If you have it in your garden, contact your local council for advice, because it must be disposed of properly. Research has shown that clumps of the weed may be contained using reinforced polythene barriers. Glyphosate applied at flowering time has some effect.

Cleavers, goosegrass
Galium aparine

This is a sprawling or climbing annual weed with sticky-hairy, fragile stems and small, white flowers that soon set seed. The seed is a tiny burr that attaches itself to anything or anyone that passes by, and so the plant spreads. It is easy enough to pull out the plants, but do so before the seed has set, otherwise the very action of trying to extricate the stems from the surrounding foliage will increase your problem at least tenfold. Chemical controls are rarely necessary.

Winter heliotrope
Petasites fragrans

Introduced as an ornamental, this coarse interloper can be a pest in gardens, spreading by means of underground runners and popping up among clumps of much more desirable specimens. It does not produce seed, because the plants brought from southern Europe were all males. Where it has spread widely, dig out as much as you possibly can and then use spot weedkiller or glyphosate on the regrowth. On the plus side, the flowers have a pleasant fragrance that is reminiscent of vanilla.

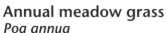

Annual meadow grass
Poa annua

By the time you notice this in your borders it will probably have long, floppy stems and a light dusting of seeds. If dealt with quickly, small patches are easy to uproot by hand or using a hand fork or hoe. Larger areas or well-established ones are more difficult to shift, since the roots spread to form a thick mat. Digging them out with a border fork is an option, though it is heavy work, or you can use a weedproof membrane to kill off the top-growth.

Lesser celandine
Ranunculus ficaria

Lesser celandine is a pretty plant of woodlands and damp hedgerows. Its shiny, dark green leaves and yellow flowers appear early in the year and then the whole plant dies down. In areas where it appears in small numbers together with spring bulbs, such as snowdrops, it could easily be tolerated.

If lesser celandine is a problem, use a spot weedkiller or treat wider areas with glyphosate. Digging out or hoeing is not recommended, since you will inevitably leave some of the tiny bulbils behind.

Buttercup
Ranunculus repens

There are several buttercup species, all variations on a theme (yellow flowers and rosettes of divided leaves), but the most annoying in gardens is creeping buttercup, which spreads by rooting runners that soon produce new plants. It is most common on damp but well-drained soils.

Individuals are easy to dig up with a hand fork or dandelion grubber. Use a hoe to uproot them on well-cultivated soil. Large areas can be dealt with using glyphosate. On lawns, a weed-and-feed application (*see* pages 50–1) should do the trick.

Broad-leaved dock
Rumex obtusifolius

Docks have large, paddle-shaped leaves and unremarkable green flowers that dry to a rust red as the seeds mature. In gardens the plants are often solitary or in small patches and not much of a problem. However, they are not very attractive and they also act as hosts to a range of soil pests, including potato eelworm, so they are best removed.

On very loose soil, a gentle, slow pull might succeed in removing the whole tap root. Otherwise, resort to weekly removal of top-growth or use a spot weedkiller.

Groundsel
Senecio vulgaris

Where it likes the conditions – fertile, loose soil – this annual weed rapidly covers both open and occupied ground. Individual plants can flower continuously for several months, which means that seeds are produced almost all the year round. The plant acts as a host for rusts and rots, so it should be removed whenever it is seen. Luckily, this is an easy job: it can be pulled up by hand or using a hand fork. Regular hoeing will keep it in check. Chemicals should not be necessary.

Common chickweed
Stellaria media

A low-growing annual with lax, spreading stems bearing small leaves and even tinier white flowers, chickweed seems to seed itself very quickly, particularly on fertile soil, rapidly becoming widespread.

Regular hoeing will prevent plants from taking hold. Where they have become established, uproot them using a border fork; smaller areas can be dug out with a hand fork. Ease out as many roots as possible, as they may regrow from any that remain. On lawns, regular mowing should do for it.

Dandelion
Taraxacum officinale
The flowers of the dandelion might be cheerful, but should be removed on sight to prevent the seeds from developing, which happens very quickly. One of the great gardening skills is removing a dandelion root whole using a grubber (*see* page 30): ease it down the side of the root to the base, then gently slide out the root. It is possible on loose, well-dug soil, but often a piece of root is left and you get two plants where there was one. Spot weedkiller, applied several times, is a reasonable alternative, particularly on lawns.

Stinging nettle
Urtica dioica, U. urens
This plant needs no introduction. There are annual and perennial varieties and both sting equally effectively; on the plus side, they do indicate that your soil is fertile. Nettles are best dug out when young, before the roots have had a chance to spread, because they produce new stems wherever they break the soil surface. Large patches are easier to tackle in winter, when the stems have died down – the roots are yellow, so quite obvious. Weedproof membrane or glyphosate may be a less strenuous option.

Speedwell
Veronica persica
There are annual and perennial species of speedwell, and this is an annual. It is a pity it is so straggly and irritating, because the flowers are pretty and beautifully marked. Don't be tempted to ignore it though, since it seeds extremely effectively, and the stems root too. Digging out or hoeing is hard work because of the density of the roots, and anything left will resprout. Use weedproof membrane or glyphosate on large patches. Other speedwell species can be a problem on lawns (*see* page 55).

Deceptive ornamentals

By now you will have a good idea of the types of plants that you might find growing in your garden without invitation and what to do about them. But there is another group that can be even more insidious: plants that you have actually chosen to include. There are quite a few ornamentals that, given the conditions they like, can reveal a more thuggish side to their nature. It pays to be aware of these characters before you given them bed room.

Periwinkle (*Vinca*) spreads by sending out long, slender stems that root when the end touches the ground, soon forming a dense mat.

Creepers

Creepers sneakily inveigle their way into nooks and crannies, and before you know it have taken up residence all around the garden. Creeping Jenny (*Lysimachia nummularia* 'Aurea') grows roots at every leaf axil, and when you pull it up the slender stems snap where they have rooted, ensuring its survival. Put it in the garden and you will have it for life; the same goes for the tiny-leaved mind-your-own-business (*Soleirolia soleirolii*): so innocent-looking but so very persistent.

Of course, such plants have their place. The creeping *Campanula poscharskyana* and *Campanula portenschlagiana* are valued for their ability to grow on walls, where their pretty blue flowers and serrated leaves disguise any amount of ugly masonry, although they will wander elsewhere given the chance.

Most gardeners know to be wary of ivies (*Hedera*), though many of the cultivated varieties are not a great problem, but all too often bamboos are allowed to get a foothold and then run riot. Most really must be restricted when they are planted, otherwise their rooting rhizomes – like the canes but horizontal – will spread, and they are extremely tough and very difficult to dig up. They will fill not only your garden, but also the one next door and any banks or spaces in between.

Self-seeders

Self-seeders are slightly less of a nuisance than creepers, since they spread only once a year – at seeding time. However, at this point they really can spread. Each plant is capable of producing a huge quantity of offspring and these can get a surprising distance away from their parents before germinating. One of their best moves is from spent flowerheads in the compost heap to new parts of the garden in

Other creeping, seeding and clumping plants

CREEPERS
Ajuga reptans (bugle)
Cerastium tomentosum (snow-in-summer)
Fallopia baldschuanica (mile-a-minute)
Galium odoratum (sweet woodruff)
Phalaris arundinacea var. *picta* (gardener's garters, ribbon grass)
Vinca major, V. minor (periwinkle)

SELF-SEEDERS
Alchemilla mollis (lady's mantle)
Borago officinalis (borage)
Carex pendula (pendulous sedge)
Geranium × *oxonianum, G. psilostemon*
Myosotis (forget-me-not)
Oenothera biennis (evening primrose)
Origanum vulgare (wild marjoram)
Papaver rhoeas, P. somniferum (poppies)
Tanacetum parthenium 'Aureum' (golden feverfew)

CLUMPERS
Achillea filipendulina (yarrow)
Anemone hupehensis (Japanese anemone)
Crocus tommasinianus
Lamium maculatum (dead nettle)
Symphytum officinale (comfrey)

At their very best when seen *en masse*, field poppies (*Papaver rhoeas*) can be prolific self-seeders, like most annual poppies. However, the seedlings are easy to spot and remove anywhere they are not wanted.

well-rotted compost. Fortunately, many self-seeders are easy to remove through weeding, and the more relaxed gardener will allow some seedlings to grow to maturity. If you don't want them to seed, remove the flowerheads before the seeds have set, although in some cases this means foregoing part of the plant's attraction. A word of warning, too: sometimes seed-setting is earlier than you think. Quaking grass (*Briza*), for instance, seems capable of growing from very green seeds.

Clumpers

In theory, any clump-forming plant could become a nuisance, but in practice only a few do, and this is usually because of some other facet of their character. For example, pretty blue grape hyacinths (*Muscari armeniacum*) spread widely, but it is their limp, grassy foliage that is their downfall. *En masse* they look untidy and unattractive, so they need regular digging up and splitting. The most widespread montbretia, *Crocosmia × crocosmiiflora*, grows in thick clumps of corms and eventually crowds even itself out. This is the most commonly seen variety, partly because in the past gardeners, fed up with its vigorous habit, have chucked it out into the countryside. Decades later, its flowers turn hedgerows and banks to a blaze of orange in late summer.

The wary gardener

If a friendly neighbour offers you armfuls of a plant dug from their garden, think twice before accepting it into your garden, as it might be a bit of a thug. It sounds rather cynical, but why else have they got plenty to give away? Thank them for their generosity, but check on the plant's behaviour before planting. Try looking over a few fences to see whether it's around in other people's gardens and what it's doing there. Remember, sometimes a plant that grows in a controlled way in one garden can be badly behaved in another.

Grape hyacinths (*Muscari*) have lovely flowers but they spread quickly and have sprawling leaves.

Lawns

Even in this age of ever-smaller gardens, most of us still want a lawn. Nevertheless, when we have one, we often don't look after it properly. Lawns are frequently overused and underfed; they are lumpy, bumpy and patchy, and then we complain that they always need mowing. And yet, a well-tended lawn is the crowning glory of the garden, providing the stage around which all your precious ornamentals can perform, and making an attractive surface for walking and sitting on.

Why do lawns have problems?

Lawns are not natural and like any other plant grasses need care in order to thrive. Think of wild landscapes that consist of grass plants: moorlands, meadows, savannahs, prairies. In these, the grass is usually rough and tussocky, with long and short bits and masses of other plants growing in between. It is rarely the smooth, rich green sward consisting of just three or four species that we want in our gardens. There are two main causes of lawn problems: neglect and being badly laid in the first place.

This is a classic neglected lawn with bare patches and yellowing grass. However, it would not take very long to transform it.

Badly laid lawns

Many lawns come into being almost by default, without any real thought being given to their requirements or the needs of their users. The ground is not properly prepared and the choice of grass species is haphazard. No attention is paid to whether the grass likes the conditions it is expected to grow in: poor drainage and shade are not good for grass health, for instance. If you're laying a lawn from scratch, make sure you dig over the site thoroughly, add soil improvers if necessary and level the site, raking to remove surface stones. Choose the grass-seed mix or turf type carefully – hardwearing, shady and drought-tolerant mixes are all good choices if you haven't got time to maintain a luxury lawn.

Neglected lawns

Grass should be treated as a high-performance plant – sensitive, delicate and demanding. However, many gardeners neglect their lawn, so it consists more of weeds than grass and any grass that does grow is sickly and nutrient-starved. We don't mow it as often as we should, then mow it too short, and, to add insult to injury, we stand on the lawn while tending to the inmates of the flower beds, compacting its soil and damaging its edges. Try to carry out a regular maintenance routine (see pages 46–9) and problems will be greatly reduced.

Considering the alternatives

If you have an unattractive, weed-filled lawn, you can do something about it (see pages 50–1), but you might also like to consider whether a lawn is the best choice for your garden and your needs. Small lawns, in particular, are very difficult to maintain and keep healthy, and a sickly lawn is highly visible in a small garden. In a restricted space, hard landscaping, such as paving, brickwork, gravel and decking, can be a good alternative and, though expensive to install, much less work in the long run. Use hard materials sensibly and sensitively. Don't pave over the whole garden, but rather leave spaces for decorative detailing, such as gravel and plants (right). Decking (far right) is an attractive, low-maintenance choice that comes in a range of styles and prices.

Maintaining a lawn

Plants are extremely forgiving, none more so than grass. When you tackle a neglected lawn, you can see positive improvements in it almost immediately, and a routine of seasonal tasks is the best way to get your grass back on track. If your lawn is badly sited, poorly laid or damaged, it will need more renovation work, but it is possible to turn even a disaster area into a lovely green sward. Problems like overgrown edges, lumps, dips and worn-out patches are all fairly straightforward. Poor drainage may need more drastic measures.

Mow in dry weather and cut little and often, to keep the grass healthy and before weeds start to grow. Never remove more than one third of the grass in any one cut.

Weeding and feeding

Like any other plant, grass needs food. Its food-making organs – the leaves – are constantly being removed through mowing, so you could argue it needs food more than most plants. It definitely needs plenty of nitrogen for leafy growth and it will respond very gratefully to a good feed.

Traditionally, lawns are fed at least twice a year – in the spring and in the autumn. Many lawn specialists like to feed every six weeks during the summer months as well. Lawn-feed manufacturers make products that are specially formulated for the

season, giving them obvious names such as 'Spring Feed' and 'Autumn Feed'. Spring feeds are higher in nitrogen than autumn feeds, the reason being that you don't want to promote lots of lush, frost-vulnerable growth at the end of the year.

Many lawn feeds are formulated as a combination with a weed- and/or moss killer, making them convenient to use on a neglected lawn. If you have scruples about using these chemicals, there are also organic feeds available, based on ingredients like seaweed or bonemeal, but these will not kill weeds.

Feeds are usually applied as granules or a powder and need to be scattered evenly over the grass. Do this on a day when rain is

imminent or water them in yourself, otherwise scorching can occur.

Mowing

Never underestimate the importance of mowing on the state of your lawn, and always have sharp cutting blades. Mowing helps to kill off some lawn weeds as well as keeping the grass in good condition. Never cut closer than 1.2cm (½in), since this removes too much of the leaf blade, but try not to allow it to get longer than 3cm (1½in), which will make it difficult to mow and more likely to look yellow after mowing and allow weeds and coarser grasses to take hold. Don't mow when the ground is wet, and as far as possible remove the clippings.

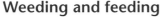

Don't forget

Seed is best sown in late summer or early autumn, or in late spring. Turf can be laid any time when the weather is fine.

Edging

To keep edges tidy, trim them at least once a week while the grass is actively growing, and preferably each time the grass is mown. You should also aim to re-cut the edges once a year. If your lawn edges are very neglected, you may have to decide where they actually need to go. Mark them up using a length of string or a plank for straight edges; curves can be created with a hose and the shapes marked out using sand. Once you know where you're going, edging is simply a case of working around the edges of the lawn using a half-moon cutter. Slice vertically down through the turf to create a crisp line of earth. You may need to repair broken edges and re-seed (*see* right).

Regular trimming of the lawn edges keeps them neat and prevents the grass spreading into the flower beds.

HOW TO repair a broken edge

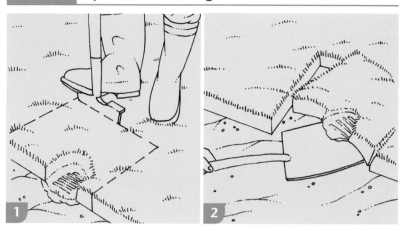

1 Cut a square or rectangular shape in the turf to encompass the damaged area. A half-moon cutter will give a neater edge than the curved blade of a spade.

2 Carefully undercut the turf at a depth of about 6cm (2½in). Free the cut section and slide it forward, moving the damaged area beyond the lawn edge.

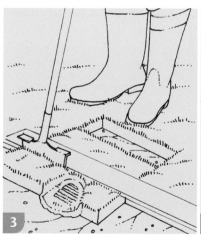

3 Using a wooden batten or plank as a guide for a straight cut, neatly slice off the damaged section in line with the edge of the lawn.

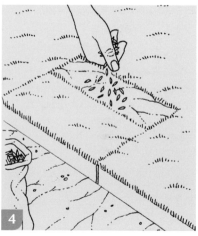

4 Press the remaining piece of turf into place and fill the gap in the lawn behind it with soil. Re-seed it with a grass-seed mix similar to the rest of the lawn. Water well.

Preventing drought

For most of the year, grass should get enough water from rainfall. However, it may suffer during prolonged dry periods in summer. There are drought-resistant grass varieties available, and you can introduce them gradually by overseeding. It is rarely practical to water the whole lawn, especially as hosepipe bans are now common, but it is wise to water patches you know dry out. You can also reduce water loss by setting the mower on a higher cut and leaving the clippings on the lawn, but do this only in very hot, dry weather.

Annual maintenance

Apart from regular mowing and feeding, lawns need to be given an annual makeover to improve growing conditions and ensure the continued health of the grass.

Scarifying

As the season progresses, lawns build up an underlayer known as thatch, which consists of dead grass and other plant material. It sits around the grass leaves and slowly chokes them, encouraging fungal infections and moss growth. Scarifying is the way to get rid of it and is best done in the autumn.

Using a spring-tine rake, work through the grass in one direction, removing all the debris that the tines pull up. Once you have finished, go back and rake at right angles to your first direction. You'll be amazed at just how much more comes up. Scarifying can be a hard job, so do a bit at a time if necessary.

Use a spring-tine rake to scarify the lawn once a year. This involves removing moss and thatch.

Making small holes in your lawn with a garden fork improves drainage, eases compaction and allows air to get to the grass roots.

Aerating

Next on the list is aerating, sometimes called spiking. This is making little holes in the lawn, which enables air to get into the soil and improves water drainage. Compaction is a problem on lawns because they are walked all over and never dug, so think of aerating as the lawn's version of annual digging.

Using a border fork or a special aerating tool with hollow tines, work over the lawn, driving the tines in by about 7–10cm (3–4in) every 15–20cm (6–8in) or so. Again, this is hard work, so do the worst bits first, such as around flower beds, play areas or the washing line. Mechanical aerators can be hired for large lawns.

Top-dressing

Finally comes top-dressing, which involves covering the lawn with a thin layer of mixed, good-quality topsoil (loam), peat-free multi-purpose compost and sand. This provides the grass with new rooting opportunities as well as improving the lawn's drainage and fertility and filling in small dips and holes. It is a bit of a fiddly job, which means it is often avoided, but if you make the time you'll see the benefits. Apply the right mix for your soil (*see* box, below) a bit at a time, using the back of a rake to spread it over the grass and into holes. When you are finished you should still be able to see the tops of the grass blades.

You can overseed at the same time, adding grass seed to the top-dressing at half the rate for sowing a new lawn. Not only does this help thicken up your lawn, it also lets you introduce a tougher or more drought-tolerant type of grass without starting from scratch.

Top-dressing mixes

Mix the top-dressing according to the soil in your garden. You will need about 1.3kg (3lb) per square metre (11 square feet) of lawn. Use sharp sand and a fine garden sieve to get rid of lumps.

HEAVY SOIL	1 part peat-free compost: 2 parts loam: 4 parts sand
LOAMY SOIL	1 part peat-free compost: 4 parts loam: 2 parts sand
LIGHT SOIL	2 parts peat-free compost: 4 parts loam: 1 part sand

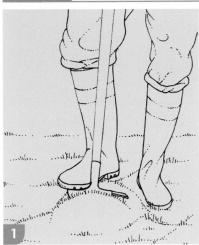

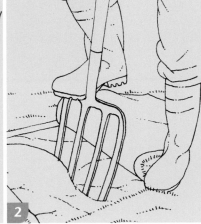

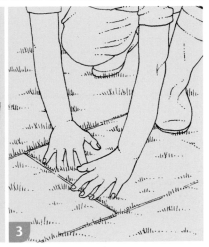

Excavate the area, peeling back the turf if necessary. Do this by cutting an H-shape across the top of the dip or bump and then undercutting the turf to reveal the soil.

Loosen and remove any problem or excess soil from bumpy areas, or add new topsoil to hollows until the patch is level with the surrounding lawn.

Roll the turf back into place, checking that it is completely flat, and adjust the level if necessary. Press it down, sift soil into any cracks, and water thoroughly.

Lawn problems

Over time, lawns develop problem areas. Underlying conditions or surface traffic cause undulations, and scruffy, bald patches appear.

Bumps and hollows

Lawns that are poorly laid may have large stones, builder's rubble, pieces of wood or other rubbish close to the surface. Over the years these can create lumps or dips in the lawn, and such areas often have poor grass growth. They may dry out very quickly in summer or become waterlogged very quickly when it rains, so it is important to remove any debris as far as possible.

Bare patches

Grass often disappears from areas that are very well used or that have had something spilt on them; always fill the petrol tank of the lawnmower on a hard surface to avoid adding to your problems. When you treat large areas of weeds (*see* page 50) you may also be left with bare patches.

With heavily used areas, consider whether an alternative surface might be more appropriate. For example, if you have a well-worn track to the garden shed, a path following the same route might be a sensible investment; where the kids play ball, grass-reinforcement mats could be the answer. Where the problem is contamination, dig out the affected soil and dispose of it sensibly, then refill the area with fresh soil. Before re-seeding any bare patches, rake the area flat, then sow grass seed thinly. Water well and cover the seed bed with netting, fleece or loose-weave hessian to protect it from birds while it is germinating.

If you prefer to use turf, remove a square or rectangular area of soil the size of your piece of turf. Lightly fork over the surface underneath and water well before placing the turf.

Improving lawn drainage

Good drainage is essential for a healthy lawn. Clay soil is more likely to be poorly drained than sand, and low-lying gardens near the water table will experience more problems than those on slopes.

Where drainage is poor due to the underlying soil structure, it is worth hiring a mechanical aerator, which will do a good job of decompacting the top few centimetres. A more drastic course of action is to dig drains or make a soakaway system to encourage the water to drain away more quickly. On a flat site, a soakaway system is the best solution. However, it will involve starting from scratch and removing the lawn entirely. Where the land slopes slightly, simple drains can be dug so long as there is an existing drainage system to which they can be connected. Again, the lawn will have to be sacrificed.

Dealing with weeds and moss

Because lawns are wide, open, usually sunny areas that are perfect for seed germination, they almost inevitably contain weeds. These can grow and spread quite quickly, but moss, often thought of as a plant of damp and shady places, is even more common on lawns. It is usually more widespread too, and it can be very persistent. A regular maintenance routine is the best way to keep weed numbers in check, while also keeping on top of moss.

Common in damp lawns, self-heal has pretty, purple-blue flowers, so might be tolerated; if not, it is easy to dig it out.

Weeds

Many weeds enjoy much the same conditions as grass (*see* pages 52–5). For some, regular mowing is enough to keep them under control, but will rarely eradicate them; for others, you will need to be more proactive.

Patches of weeds

If your lawn has just a few patches of weeds, the best approach – and the most environmentally friendly – is to dig them out, removing the roots as far as possible and then re-seed the area with grass. While the grass seedlings are still young and thin, keep an eye out for regrowing or germinating weeds among them, and ease these out. Once the grass has grown and knitted together to cover the bare soil, new weeds are less likely to germinate.

Where weeds are in ones or twos, a spot weedkiller that kills weeds but not grass is quicker and easier, if you have no reservations about using one. Contact killers will kill the top-growth, and during the growing season this might be enough to allow the grass to move in and fill the area; otherwise use a systemic herbicide. If you plan to kill off large areas of weeds with a herbicide, allow six weeks before re-seeding. Again, keep an eye on the bare patch during this time and remove any weedy regrowth before it gets too well established.

Widespread weeds

For large areas of weedy lawn or where you need to feed the grass too, use lawn sand (*see* page 59) or a weed-and-feed treatment. These have been shown to be better than just using straight weedkillers. Sprinkle the granules or powder evenly over the lawn on a day when rain is expected to prevent the grass from scorching. A manually operated distributor, available from garden centres, will make this easier.

Moss

Moss spreads through a lawn almost imperceptibly, until the whole sward is full of its bright green stems. You might tolerate its presence if you consider only overall appearance, because from a distance the 'grass' certainly looks good. However, moss chokes grass and for those of us who like our lawns healthy, its presence is not welcome.

Dandelions are persistent in lawns and elsewhere. However, deft use of a dandelion grubber may do the trick.

A carefully directed squirt with a contact weedkiller should be effective where digging up is not easy.

Unlike weeds, which are simply opportunistic space fillers, moss is a symptom of a wider problem with the underlying growing conditions. To eradicate the moss, you need to identify and deal with the cause. You could rake it out or resort to using a moss killer, both of which might get rid of it temporarily, but if nothing else changes, the moss will return when the conditions are right, mainly in spring or autumn.

If necessary, you can use liquid weedkillers to treat large patches of weeds on lawns. Use them on a dry, still day in spring or early summer.

Causes and cures

Poor growing conditions, such as infertile soil or very dry soil through the summer, can lead to the growth of moss. If this is the case, the standard lawn-maintenance routine will make inroads into the problem. Pay attention to watering during long, dry spells too.

At the other end of the scale, waterlogging and insufficient drainage are also common problems that encourage moss growth, as is compacted soil. These often go together anyway. Aerating (*see* page 48) is a good first step, but if this is unsuccessful, consider undertaking further work to improve drainage (*see* page 49).

Another reason moss grows in lawns is scalping (*see* page 57). This is when the mower cuts the grass too short, sometimes revealing the soil below, and often occurs at border edges. With scalping, the only solution is to mow more carefully.

Shady areas are more likely to be mossy too. Here you could try a shade-tolerant grass mix, or go with the flow and forget about having grass at all. Shade-loving plants, bark mulch or a hard surface (*see* page 45) are good options.

Finally, moss can be more widespread where the soil is too acidic, although this is reasonably rare. If a pH test shows the soil is acidic, you could add lime to counteract the acidity. Do not lime without checking, because alkaline soil will also create problems, such as encouraging wormcasts.

Gallery of lawn weeds and diseases

Yarrow

There are many weeds that will grow in lawns. Different species tend to favour different growing conditions and so will be more prevalent in some regions than in others. Those shown here are the more common varieties; they are all perennial unless otherwise stated. Diseases and other lawn problems, usually caused by growing conditions, are covered on pages 56–7.

Weeds and moss

Although there are a few weeds that are regularly found in both lawns and flower beds, in general those that flourish in lawns tend to have particular growth habits: they are low-growing and spreading and, obviously, don't mind a regular drastic haircut. They can be very persistent, partly because it can be difficult to dig them out completely from among the grass roots, but also because they will have left plenty of seed behind and this quickly germinates to refill any bare areas. As with weeds in flower beds, digging out should still be the first resort, and weedkillers the last.

Parsley-piert

Yarrow
Achillea millefolium

When you see yarrow that has not been mown, it is difficult to believe this tall, almost stately plant with its masses of soft, feathery, carrot-like leaves could survive in a close-cropped lawn, but it does. It spreads by stems that root as they go and is definitely tough.
PREVENTION AND CONTROL It is hard to get rid of except by persistent digging up, since it is fairly resistant to weedkilling chemicals. If you do not want to dig, revisit the spot with a selective weedkiller at least twice.

Parsley-piert
Aphanes arvensis

Parsley-like leaves give this little annual weed its common name. It also has tiny, green flowers, although these are hardly distinguishable from the rest of the plant. The stems grow rapidly, creeping through the grass and quickly becoming so entangled that digging out is a challenge.

PREVENTION AND CONTROL Feeding the lawn diligently will prevent parsley-piert from thriving; if it has already taken hold, use a selective weedkiller if necessary. Setting the mower on a higher cut can help, since short grass gives this weed a chance to grow.

Daisy
Bellis perennis

Daisies are common in lawns, and are tolerated by many gardeners. Their ground-hugging rosettes of spoon-shaped, toothed leaves easily duck under the lawnmower blades, and you know you should be cutting the lawn when the flowers start to decorate the grass.
PREVENTION AND CONTROL Daisies are usually quite small plants and easy to dig up, so there is no excuse for letting them spread. Once they have done, it might be quicker to use a selective weedkiller. One treatment is usually sufficient. Lawn sand (*see* page 59) will reduce the vigour of the plants.

Daisy

Mouse-ear chickweed
Cerastium holosteoides

This hairy-leaved weed is very common on lawns, its hairs giving it a silvery appearance. It has tiny, white flowers at the top of stems that stick up above its dense mats of flat, creeping foliage.
PREVENTION AND CONTROL The plants can spread widely, which makes them difficult to dig out. They self-seed very efficiently too. Use lawn sand in spring to check their vigour (*see* page 59). If necessary, use selective weedkiller later in the year.

Smooth hawk's beard
Crepis capillaris

This low, spreading annual weed is very similar to cat's ear (*Hypochaeris radicata*), with a rosette of narrow, dandelion-like leaves and thin flower stalks carrying small, yellow, dandelion-like flowers.
PREVENTION AND CONTROL Prevent seeding by regular mowing to remove the flowerheads. Dig up rosettes as soon as you see them. Although they have a tap root, they are not very persistent. Use a spot weedkiller as a last resort.

Cat's ear
Hypochaeris radicata

This has flat rosettes of serrated-edged, reasonably fleshy leaves, each produced by a single, long tap root. The small, dandelion-like flowers sit on the top of wiry, branching stems. It spreads by seed.
PREVENTION AND CONTROL Digging out is difficult because any tap root left behind will regrow. If using weedkiller, several applications will be needed. Hawkbits and hawkweeds look similar but are less common; dig them out or treat with a spot weedkiller.

Bird's-foot trefoil
Lotus corniculatus

Also called bacon and eggs, this is a low-growing plant with clover-like leaves and yellow, two-lipped flowers variably streaked with red. The flower buds are usually more heavily marked with red. Although its stems are wide-spreading, each plant has a single, deep tap root; it spreads by seed. Black medick (*Medicago lupulina*) looks similar but has very small, yellow flowerheads.
PREVENTION AND CONTROL They can be difficult to dig out cleanly, but this is the best approach as they are quite resistant to selective weedkillers.

Black medick
Medicago lupulina

Usually a nuisance only in neglected lawns, this annual or short-lived perennial weed is superficially similar to clover (*Trifolium repens*), with trefoil leaves and small, rounded flowerheads. The flowers are yellow turning to black as the seeds ripen. It has a thin, wiry tap root.
PREVENTION AND CONTROL Unlike those of clover, the stems do not root, so this weed is fairly easy to dig out where it occurs in small patches, but may resprout. Over a wider area, you might resort to a spot weedkiller, but will need to make at least two applications.

Other lawn weeds

The following lawn weeds are featured in the Gallery of garden weeds:
Annual meadow grass (page 39)
Buttercup (page 39)
Common chickweed (page 40)
Couch grass (page 37)
Creeping thistle (page 36)
Dandelion (page 41)

Mouse-ear chickweed

Cat's ear

Bird's-foot trefoil

Plantain
Plantago major, P. media, P. lanceolata

The plantains are quite distinctive, with comparatively large, ribbed, oval, pointed leaves. The leaves of many species are similar to hosta foliage, hence the hosta's other common name of plantain lily.
PREVENTION AND CONTROL There are three plantains common in lawns – greater, hoary and ribwort; all can be dug out fairly easily when young and in small patches. Because they are relatively large, you should spot them as soon as they appear and be able to deal with them straightaway. There should be no need to resort to chemicals, although these are very effective against them.

Knotgrass
Polygonum aviculare

This annual weed is an occasional problem in areas where the lawn is very well used, because it thrives in compacted ground. It has thick-textured, elongated-oval leaves and spreading, reddish stems. The flowers are tiny and pink or white.
PREVENTION AND CONTROL Where there are only one or two plants, digging up is the best option. Aerate, feed and water the lawn regularly to get rid of the compaction. Knotgrass is easily killed by selective weedkillers.

Creeping cinquefoil
Potentilla reptans

This rosette-forming plant is most likely to be found growing from lawn edges into flower beds, or the other way around. It creeps a long way on thin but tough, rooting stems and has strawberry-like leaves of five leaflets with toothed edges, and yellow flowers on individual stems.

PREVENTION AND CONTROL Where creeping cinquefoil has taken hold in the lawn, rake up the stems before mowing to ensure you remove as much as possible. It is very difficult to dig up, since it leaves plenty of stem and root behind. Use a weedkiller as a last resort; you will need at least two applications.

Self-heal
Prunella vulgaris

Self-heal is a pretty plant that is welcomed in wildflower meadows, with purple-blue flowers in groups at the top of a stalk. The leaves are oval and bright green.
PREVENTION AND CONTROL In lawns self-heal can be a disfigurement, but it is easily dug out. Larger patches will succumb to an annual treatment with lawn sand (*see* page 59), so other weedkillers should not be necessary unless the problem is widespread. It tends to favour damp lawns, so try to improve drainage. (*See also* page 49.)

Sheep's sorrel
Rumex acetosella

A creeping weed that can be a persistent nuisance in lawns, sheep's sorrel has arrowhead-shaped, often grey-green leaves with two small lobes at the base. The leaves taste sour and are used in a herbal tea. It can produce a spike of tiny, green flowers that turn red, but it rarely flowers in lawns.
PREVENTION AND CONTROL Where it has taken hold in the lawn, rake up the stems before mowing to ensure you remove as much as possible. Sheep's sorrel is very difficult to dig up, since it leaves plenty of stem and root behind. Use a weedkiller as a last resort; you will need at least two applications.

Plantain

Self-heal

Pearlwort

Pearlwort
Sagina procumbens

A creeping weed that forms large mats of stems and tiny, narrow leaves, pearlwort can be mistaken for moss because of its similar appearance and habit. It can be a nuisance, especially in better-quality lawns consisting of finer grasses that are regularly closely mown.
PREVENTION AND CONTROL If you catch it early, it is possible to dig out small patches, but otherwise use a selective weedkiller. Lawn sand (*see* page 59) will reduce its spread and vigour. It is not very persistent, so one treatment should be sufficient.

Clover
Trifolium repens

Clover is a well-established grass weed. However, a small-leaved clover variety is now used as part of a drought-resistant lawn mix. Known as microclover, it also smothers other weeds and can be cut with a lawnmower. In all-grass lawns, though, normal-size clover can be a nuisance, particularly on alkaline or neutral soil. Its stems root as they spread, making digging up very difficult.
PREVENTION AND CONTROL Rake the grass before mowing so that the long stems are pulled up and cut as well. Use lawn sand to reduce its vigour (*see* page 59) and weed-and-feed in spring.

Germander speedwell
Veronica chamaedrys

This is a hairy little plant with oval foliage that has indented edges. The leaves are arranged opposite each other on the sprawling stems. The four-petalled flowers are similar to those of round-leaved speedwell but bluer.

PREVENTION AND CONTROL
Germander is not as common as round-leaved speedwell, but it can be difficult to remove, since the stems root along their length. This habit also makes spot weedkillers ineffective. Lawn sand (*see* page 59) can help.

Round-leaved speedwell
Veronica filiformis

This delicate-looking plant, with sky-blue flowers, was introduced as an ornamental and made itself at home, thriving in both sun and shade. It spreads by creeping stems, and mowing distributes fragments of stem across the lawn to take root, so it is essential to remove clippings to control it. Speedwell is not usually much of a problem in healthy lawns.
PREVENTION AND CONTROL Feeding the lawn, leaving the grass a bit longer and hand-pulling patches that do appear are often the most effective remedies; weedkillers rarely control it unless the lawn is in good health too.

Mosses

The three main lawn varieties of moss indicate different problems. Upright moss is found in dry lawns on acid soil. It has long stems that stick up beside and through the grass. Trailing moss is widespread in shady or damp areas and has thick, lax stems. It forms clumps, as does cushion moss, which often appears on scalped areas and has short, densely packed upright stems.
PREVENTION AND CONTROL Regular lawn maintenance (*see* pages 50–1) will reduce moss invasions. Use moss killer, but where poor drainage or heavy shade are the causes these need to be addressed. Lawn sand (*see* page 59) will reduce the vigour of the plants.

Clover

Round-leaved speedwell

Upright moss

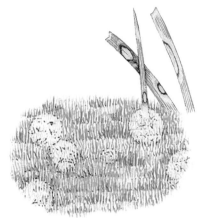

Algae

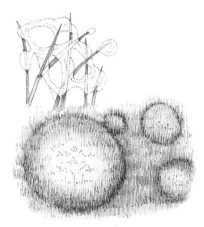

Dollar spot

Fusarium patch

Lichen

Diseases and other problems

Grasses are usually robust, disease-resistant plants that grow well in a variety of soils. However, they can still suffer from problems and some of the finer-leaved species in particular are prone to disease, often because we are trying to grow them under conditions in which they would not normally thrive. The diseases and disorders featured here are much less likely to occur or cause widespread damage on well-maintained lawns. Many originate from the condition of the soil itself – as always, keeping your soil healthy is a good way to ensure you keep your plants healthy too.

Algae

On lawns, algae usually appear as a slimy green substance coating the soil, but where it has dried out it can also be black and crispy. It can make the area quite slippery. Algae are particularly common on waterlogged areas, but may also grow where the grass is patchy.

PREVENTION AND CONTROL Regular aeration and top-dressing (*see* page 48) are the best treatments, since you cannot dig algae out. Moss killers will get rid of the problem but only temporarily. If the algae occur in a shady area, under trees for example, it might be better to consider an alternative ground covering rather than grass (*see* pages 45 and 51), because you are unlikely to be able to improve conditions enough to get rid of the problem for good.

Dollar spot

Small, round, yellow patches on the lawn are usually the first indication of this fungal disease. If you look more closely at the grass, you will see yellow, spotted areas on the blades, which are turning brown and then dying. Dollar spot is more common on lawns of fine grasses, and most particularly attacks creeping red fescue (widely used in turf grass).

PREVENTION AND CONTROL A good lawn-maintenance programme makes this disease much less likely to strike: water during dry spells and feed properly. A spring feed is particularly beneficial. Scarify and aerate the whole area every autumn (*see* page 48).

Fusarium patch

Also known as snow mould, this is a fungal infection caused by the sort of damp, cool conditions in which all fungi thrive. It kills off circular areas of grass and on dewy mornings you might see a white or pink, cobwebby growth hanging from the blades. It particularly affects areas of annual meadow grass (*Poa annua, see* page 39) and is worse where grass is walked on during frosty weather.

PREVENTION AND CONTROL Improve your lawn-maintenance routine to keep the damage to a minimum (*see* pages 46–9). Be careful not to overuse nitrogen fertilizers. Fusarium disease will disappear when the weather either dries up or warms up.

Lichen

Another indicator of neglect, lawn lichen produces growths that look a bit like dry leaves. They are dark and flat when wet and curl up when they dry, turning a lighter, greyish colour.

PREVENTION AND CONTROL Lichen is most common on shady, waterlogged lawns that are starved of nutrients.

Follow a good lawn-maintenance routine (*see* pages 46–9) to discourage their growth. Lawn sand (*see* page 59) will help, but only temporarily. If lichen continues to be a problem, consider using a different ground cover, particularly if the area is very shaded.

Mushrooms and fairy rings

Mushrooms and other small fungi will appear on most lawns from time to time. Usually, they are around for a few days before disappearing again and do not cause problems to the health of the lawn (but if eaten some can cause problems to humans). However, fairy rings are rather different. They are much more noticeable, since they create a circle of greener grass – the grass is being fed by the activities of the thread-like fungal mycelia below the surface, which break down organic material in the soil. The fruiting bodies (or mushrooms) of the fungi pop up on this circle during mushroom-growing weather.

PREVENTION AND CONTROL Feed the rest of the lawn to prevent the circles being too obvious. Pay special attention to aerating the affected grass, since the mycelia can become quite dense beneath the soil surface and the area may begin to resist water penetration, particularly after a dry spell. The only other solution is to dig out the whole area to 30cm (12in) and replace the topsoil, which is very hard work.

Ophiobolus patch

Also known as bent-grass take-all, this fungal disease troubles only grasses known as the bents (*Agrostis*) and is comparatively uncommon. It usually

occurs when the grass comes under stress, such as during a dry spell, and appears as patches of red-brown as the affected grasses start to die off. The infected areas spread and leave bare areas of lawn, in which weeds soon start to grow. If unchecked, the disease can damage large areas of grass.

PREVENTION AND CONTROL Again, the best way to avoid it taking hold is to follow good lawn-maintenance routines (*see* pages 46–9). Lawn sand (*see* page 59) may also help. Where the disease is established, it is easier to overseed with resistant grasses, such as fescues, since it will take some time to eradicate.

Red thread

Usually only fine lawn grasses, such as red fescue (*Festuca rubra*) and bents (*Agrostis*) are affected by this fungal disease, which is also known as corticium disease. However, it can also attack perennial ryegrass (*Lolium perenne*) and annual meadow grass (*Poa annua*, *see* page 39). It manifests itself as minute growths appearing on and around the grass blades and most often appears during wet weather in late summer and autumn. The first obvious signs of its presence are pale areas of lawn, as the infected grass turns pale pink; you need to look more closely to see the threads. These are only about 2mm (⅛in) long, and are pinky red and jelly-like.

PREVENTION AND CONTROL Again, this is a disease of a mismanaged lawn: follow a good maintenance routine and pay particular attention to feeding (*see* page 46). A good dose of nitrogen in the form of sulphate of ammonia may be all that is needed to control a small attack. Fortunately, this disease does not kill the grass, but it is unsightly while it lasts.

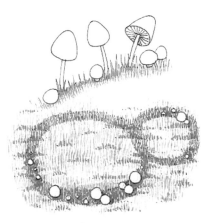

Mushrooms and fairy rings

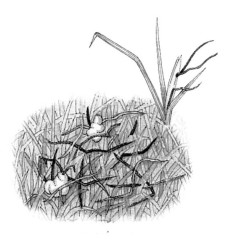

Red thread

Careless mowing

Two common problems are caused by poor mowing techniques.

Scalping often occurs when one side of the mower slips off the lawn into the flower beds. The lowered blades then remove all the grass, leaving a bare patch. High areas within the lawn may also get scalped. Remove lumps (*see* page 49) and top-dress and water other scalped areas to help the grass recover. Take your time when mowing edges.

A ripple effect across the lawn, or washboarding, is caused by always mowing in the same direction. Regularly change the direction in which you mow to avoid it. Top-dress the lawn in autumn to remove the ripples (*see* page 48).

Animal and insect pests

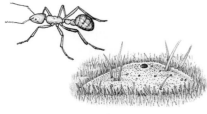
Ant

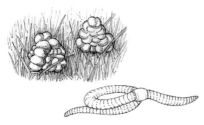
Earthworm

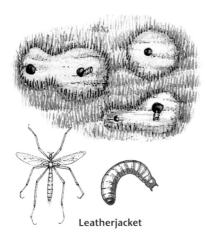

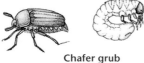
Chafer grub

Leatherjacket

Even when you are diligently looking after your lawn, it is vulnerable to a range of animal and insect attacks. The majority will affect small areas, but since you are now rather proud of your lawn, the smallest of patches will seem intolerable. Fortunately, there are only a few problems that are difficult to contain; most can be dealt with simply by keeping up your lawn-maintenance routine.

Ants

Ants often make their presence felt in lawns where the ground is warm and undisturbed. They also cluster around and under paving and paths, spilling onto the lawn in summer when they nest.
PREVENTION AND CONTROL They are not usually too much of a problem – simply sweep the dry earth away before mowing. If they become more widespread, dig up the nest and expose the eggs for birds. Ant powders should not be used in the open garden, but a biological control can be effective (*see* page 27).

Earthworms

Loved everywhere else in the garden, earthworms can be a bit of a nuisance in lawns, since they leave little sticky piles of earth 'casts' where they work.
PREVENTION AND CONTROL These piles are like small seed beds for weeds, so remove them as soon as possible, and definitely before mowing. Sweeping the lawn when they are dry will do the trick. Where the casts are widespread, it might be worth increasing the acidity of your soil with lawn sand (*see* box, opposite).

Leatherjackets

The larvae of cranefly or daddy-long-legs, leatherjackets are probably the most troublesome lawn pest because they eat the roots of the grass, which kills off the top-growth and leaves dead patches of yellow or brown lawn. The cranefly lays its eggs among the grass roots in late summer and the larvae hatch out in the autumn to begin a long winter and spring of feasting.
PREVENTION AND CONTROL Scarifying in the autumn may bring the leatherjackets – 2.5cm (1in) legless, brown or greyish grubs – to the surface, where they will make a fine meal for birds. In the spring, when you notice yellow patches appearing (*see* left), water a small area and cover it with a black plastic sheet overnight. This brings the grubs to the surface – again, a meal for the birds. A well-fed and maintained lawn will quickly recover from limited attacks by these pests. Improving drainage will reduce their numbers. If the problem is widespread, consider using a biological control (*see* page 27) in autumn and spring; it is effective but pricey.

Chafer grubs

It can be difficult to distinguish between chafer damage and harm done by leatherjackets. However, the grubs are quite different; those of the chafer are curled into a C-shape and have legs. They are less likely to cause problems, since they are much less common.
PREVENTION AND CONTROL The biological control for leatherjackets also deals with chafers.

Mining bees

Mining bees are just one of several species of bee that like to nest in the ground. They are most common in sandy soil and are noticeable because they nest in grass and create a small mound of earth at the entrance to their burrow, a landmark for the community that lives there. The mounds can be distinguished from ant hills by the volcano-like depression in their centre.

PREVENTION AND CONTROL Mining bees are good pollinators, so unless they are present in great numbers, try to leave them alone. If a mound is in the way of mowing, scoop it up beforehand.

Moles

Most of us know that large piles of sifted earth on the top of the lawn are the workings of moles underneath. However, where the ground is wet or hard, these little furry creatures may also tunnel just below the soil surface, leaving disturbed, raised areas of grass.

PREVENTION AND CONTROL Moles are notoriously difficult to get rid of and the only really reliable methods are to use traps or poison. Both of these should be carried out by pest-control professionals, and then only if you really cannot live with them.

Rabbits

Vegetable gardens are particularly targeted by rabbits, but they also like other young plants and may dig in lawns and flower beds too.

PREVENTION AND CONTROL The presence of a dog or cat in the garden may be enough to deter them. Otherwise, the only sure defence is a rabbit-proof fence, buried about 45cm

(18in) into the soil and about 1m (3ft) high. You could put one in and disguise it with planting. If the garden is too large, simply protect the vegetable plot.

Badgers and foxes

The digging activities of badgers and foxes can damage lawns, vegetable patches and flower beds. Badgers on the hunt for earthworms can root up acres of grass overnight, but they are unlikely to do so in a garden because they will be disturbed before they can go this far.

PREVENTION AND CONTROL Avoid using organic fertilizers such as blood, fish and bone, since both will be attracted to the smell. Unless the digging is very regular and destructive, the best thing to do is live with it. If you want to try to keep them out of the garden, you will need an electric fence of the mesh variety used for keeping hens safe. Even this is not guaranteed, since both animals are quite capable of digging under fences.

Dogs

Dogs also occasionally take to digging in lawns, but the most usual problem is urinating. The urine of female dogs in particular is very high in nitrogen, so where they pee the grass gets an overdose. During damp weather or in wet parts of the country, this results in very green patches that grow quickly; dry weather and dry areas will have brown markings where the excess nitrogen has scorched the grass instead.

PREVENTION AND CONTROL Soak the area immediately after the dog has peed. Try feeding a chopped tomato or tomato purée with her food – said to reduce scorching!

Mining bee

Mole

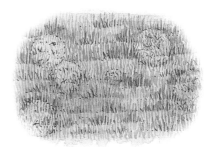

Bitch's urine

Using lawn sand

Lawn sand consists of fine sand with added weedkiller – usually ferrous (iron) sulphate, but others may be used. It can be scattered thinly on lawns in late spring or early summer, like a granular fertilizer, and settles more densely on weeds and moss, which are killed by the weedkiller. The sand is washed through to the soil, where it gradually improves drainage and aeration. Choose a dry day when rain is forecast to use lawn sand. Water the lawn well if rain does not fall within a couple of days. Don't mow for three or four days after application and do not use the first lot of grass clippings as a mulch.

Plant problems and remedies

If they're planted well in suitable conditions and given good care, most plants grow successfully, perform obligingly and suffer few problems. However, all living things endure ailments occasionally, and when they do it's good to know what's wrong, whether you need to worry about it and if there's anything that can be done.

Identifying the problem

When you see your favourite rose bush covered in aphids, or beetles munching on your treasured lilies and brown spots all over the leaves of your carefully tended broad beans, it's easy to panic and tempting to reach for a chemical spray. But don't. Take a deep breath, carefully identify the problem and assess the extent of it, and then deal with it in the most sensible way.

Understand the cause

While it's often easy to see that your plant has a problem, identifying the cause can be less straightforward. Broadly speaking, it will be one of three things: a pest, a disease or a disorder. Knowing your enemies is the first step to combating them.

What is a pest?

Gardeners are all too familiar with the bigger, obvious pests, such as slugs, aphids and caterpillars. But smaller pests, mostly insects, can cause more harm. There are many sap-sucking insects that do cosmetic damage, tiny mites that live inside leaves, grubs that hatch in fruit and eelworms that infest roots.

What is a disease?

Diseases are infections, and the most common are viruses that distort or discolour plants' leaves and fungal infections that cause spots and a range of mouldy growths. Bacterial infections, such as canker, can be very serious but, thankfully, they are quite rare.

What is a disorder?

Not every problem is caused by some hostile organism. Cold, drought or waterlogging can cause damage to leaves, flowers or fruit. Nutrient deficiencies can look like a serious disease (see page 25).

Wait it out

The simplest and least taxing of all remedies is to do nothing. Even if they look dreadful, many problems do not amount to much and do very little harm to the host plant. In some cases, there is nothing you can do – not even use a chemical cure, because there is nothing available. Some of the most successful gardeners are those who refuse to worry about a small attack of this or that, knowing that, on a generally healthy plant, its effect will be negligible in the long run.

Take action

There are actions you can take against pests and diseases knowing that nothing else will be harmed. Prune off diseased branches and stems, pick off and destroy larger pests, such as caterpillars, or squash smaller ones, such as aphids.

Biological controls can be a good option (see page 27). The drawbacks of them are that they are pricey, are available for only a limited range of problems and work only under certain circumstances.

Don't forget

Some pests and diseases are 'notifiable'. This means that if you find them you must contact your local authority or the regional FERA office, or equivalent. For more information see www.fera.defra.gov.uk.

A few pesticides and fungicides on the market contain ingredients that are not persistent and so are considered relatively environmentally friendly. These can be used in moderation, but remember, they may harm more than just the target pest or disease (see page 26).

The days of spraying with highly toxic, persistent chemicals are long gone, and the number available is steadily shrinking. Those that remain are thought to be safe when used according to the instructions, but it is vital to remember that they can harm beneficial organisms and that their long-term effects are not fully known. Only ever use them as a last resort, and double-check suitability before using them on crops.

How to use this directory

The directory that follows is divided into Ornamental plants and Vegetables and fruit. Each section is arranged according to where you are most likely to find the symptoms, although in many cases other parts of the plant will be affected too.

Ornamental plants

Adelgid

Lime nail gall

Silk button gall

When plants first sicken, the symptoms are often distinctive and confined to one or two parts. This section looks at leaf problems (pages 62–74), pond plant problems (page 75), stem and bark problems (pages 76–80), seed and cutting problems (page 81), root and plant base problems (pages 82–3), flower problems (pages 84–5) and rose problems (pages 86–9).

Tree leaf problems

Adelgids

Adelgids are sap-suckers and attack the foliage and bark of conifers. They look like black aphids covered with fluffy, white wax. In great numbers, they may cause foliage to yellow, and their excrement can encourage sooty mould (*see* page 68). Spruces may develop galls on shoot-tips.
PLANTS AFFECTED Conifers including firs (*Abies*), larch (*Larix*), pine (*Pinus*), spruce (*Picea*) and Douglas fir (*Pseudotsuga*).
HOW BAD IS IT? A heavy infestation can be disfiguring but will not affect growth unless the tree is otherwise compromised.
PREVENTION AND CONTROL In most cases, do nothing. On smaller trees, spraying with fatty acids or plant oils (*see* page 27) may be effective. As a last resort, use an approved chemical insecticide. Any treatment is best carried out in late winter, since overwintering nymphs are not covered with the protective wax.

Alder sucker

This small, hopping insect (*Psylla alni*) sucks sap from the leaf undersides and stems. It is usually green but may develop red or brown markings. Nymphs are covered with a white, fluffy, protective wax, which disappears in early summer.
PLANTS AFFECTED Alders (*Alnus*) only.
HOW BAD IS IT? Although noticeable, they are not usually a great problem.

PREVENTION AND CONTROL In most cases no action is necessary. Larger trees can shrug off attacks. Heavy infestations on small trees can be treated with pyrethrum. Spray in early summer when the protective wax has disappeared. As a last resort, use an approved chemical pesticide.

False silver leaf

Stress in the plant causes the thin, whitish membrane covering the upper leaf surface to lift, producing a silvery sheen. You can distinguish it from silver leaf disease (*see* page 97) by cutting through a stem; in false silver leaf there is no dark staining.
PLANTS AFFECTED The plum (*Prunus*) family including plums, apricots, cherries and almonds; also apples (*Malus*), poplars (*Populus*), rhododendrons and laburnums.
HOW BAD IS IT? The silvery sheen is not unattractive; once the cause is remedied, next year's leaves will return to normal.
PREVENTION AND CONTROL False silver leaf is usually caused by cultivation stress. Water well during dry spells and mulch. Use a slow-release fertilizer. Erect or plant windbreaks to protect the plant from cold.

Galls

A gall is a peculiar-looking growth on the leaves, stems or buds of a wide range of plants. The majority are harmless, though some can be a symptom of underlying problems. Most are caused by the feeding activities of tiny insects or are part of the insect's reproductive cycle. For example, the lime nail gall mite (*Eriophyes tiliae tiliae*) matures inside elongated, flame-shaped, red or white galls on the leaves of limes (*Tilia*), and the silk button gall wasp (*Neuroterus numismalis*) produces tiny, ring-like galls on oak leaves (*Quercus*), each containing a small grub.

PLANTS AFFECTED Many trees including alder (*Alnus*), crab apple (*Malus*), beech (*Fagus*), elm (*Ulmus*), gleditsia, lime (*Tilia*), mountain ash (*Sorbus*), oak (*Quercus*), pear (*Pyrus*), walnut (*Juglans*) and yew (*Taxus*). Different galls can also affect herbaceous perennials, and some shrubs including fuchsias (*see* page 68), blackcurrants (*see* page 91) and especially roses (*see* page 87), or the stems of shrubs (*see* page 77).

HOW BAD IS IT? Slightly disfiguring and some can be debilitating in the long run.

PREVENTION AND CONTROL There are no chemical controls for galls. On smaller plants or where infestations are limited, removal by hand is an option.

Horse chestnut leaf miner

White-green blotches appear between the leaf veins; these eventually turn brown. The leaves are tunnelled by the caterpillar of a small moth (*Cameraria ohridella*). The pest and its excrement can be seen in its 'mine' by holding a leaf to the light.

PLANTS AFFECTED *Aesculus hippocastanum* is most prone. *A. indica* and *A.* × *carnea* are resistant.

HOW BAD IS IT? This can be very disfiguring, but doesn't appear to affect the overall vigour of the tree, so long as it is otherwise healthy.

PREVENTION AND CONTROL Nothing can prevent attack. Remove and destroy

fallen leaves during the autumn and winter to reduce the chances of reinfestation the following year.

Willow anthracnose

This widespread fungal disease makes the leaves curl and turn yellow. They fall off the tree in early to midsummer in bad attacks. The infected leaves are often covered in tiny, dark brown spots: the spore-producing fruiting bodies. Cankers (*see* page 76) appear on the branches, usually in spring.

PLANTS AFFECTED Most serious on weeping willow (*Salix* × *sepulcralis*) and golden weeping willow (*S.* × *sepulcralis* var. *chrysocoma*).

HOW BAD IS IT? It is disfiguring, particularly if the cankers cause dieback (*see* page 78), and it weakens the tree, but rarely kills it.

PREVENTION AND CONTROL There is no way of preventing attack. Gather and destroy the fallen leaves. Prune out cankered stems at the risk of spoiling the tree's weeping shape.

Willow leaf beetle

Several different beetles, varying from metallic blue-black to brassy green-brown, attack willow leaves. Between late spring and early autumn, they eat the upper leaf surface; the exposed tissues turn brown or white as they dry out. Their larvae also feed on the leaves, sometimes *en masse*.

PLANTS AFFECTED Willows (*Salix*), birches (*Betula*) and poplars (*Populus*), including aspen (*P. tremula*).

HOW BAD IS IT? Fairly disfiguring, but only youngsters are badly affected.

PREVENTION AND CONTROL On older trees it is best to live with the problem. As a last resort on saplings, use an approved pesticide in early summer.

Horse chestnut leaf miner

Willow anthracnose

Willow leaf beetle

Leaf problems

Algae

Algae are microscopic plants that like to grow in damp conditions, near cool walls or fences and around the base of crowded shrubs or shaded trees. They may grow over both the leaf surfaces and the stems, and they also appear on bricks, pavers and wooden structures.

PLANTS AFFECTED Any growing in a damp, shady position.

HOW BAD IS IT? The green, powdery growth looks unsightly but is harmless.

PREVENTION AND CONTROL Algae can be washed or rubbed off where they are not wanted, such as on the bark of silver birches. Increasing air circulation will reduce their growth, so thin out plants or otherwise improve ventilation. Algae on hard surfaces, such as patios and paths, can be killed using various widely available algicides.

Aphids

There is an array of different aphid species, many with particular host plants, such as roses, bean plants or certain trees, which they target for raising their huge broods. As they suck sap from the plants, the aphids excrete honeydew, which is sticky and encourages black sooty moulds to grow (*see* page 68). Ants sometimes 'farm' aphids, carrying them onto new shoots and eating the sugary honeydew. Aphids are usually green, but pink, black (usually called blackfly), grey and brown species may also be seen. Woolly aphids live on stems and cover themselves with a waxy, fluffy, white substance.

PLANTS AFFECTED Almost every plant can be affected, among the most common being roses (*see* pages 86–9), nasturtiums, lupins and poppies. Fruit trees and vegetables such as broad beans are also targets (*see* page 90). Woolly aphids attack crab apples (*Malus*) and related plants such as cotoneaster and pyracantha.

HOW BAD IS IT? Aphids do not kill well-grown plants. However, they are debilitating and cause distortion of young shoots. A large infestation will kill or spoil flower buds. Aphids help to spread viruses (*see* page 74), and viruses are killers.

PREVENTION AND CONTROL Aphids have many predators, including ladybird larvae, hoverfly larvae, parasitic wasps and lacewings. Do everything you can to encourage these into your garden. Where the attack is restricted to one or two buds, regularly rub off the aphids to keep populations down. If necessary, spray with pyrethrum, soft or insecticidal soap or plant oils. As a last resort, use an approved chemical pesticide.

Bay sucker

This little aphid-like insect feeds on young leaves, causing yellowing as well as thickening and curling of the leaf margins. The damaged parts die, drying and turning brown. If you uncurl the leaf edges you will find the grey nymph inside, covered with fluffy, white wax.

PLANTS AFFECTED Sweet bay (*Laurus nobilis*) and its various coloured forms.

HOW BAD IS IT? A heavy infestation is disfiguring, particularly on clipped or potted specimens. The affected leaves do not recover.

PREVENTION AND CONTROL On larger plants the damage is not too noticeable. With smaller specimens, pick off affected leaves as far as possible. As a last resort, use an approved insecticide as soon as you spot the leaves beginning to curl.

Blackfly (aphid)

Greenfly (aphid)

Bay sucker

Berberis sawfly

Adult sawflies are not a problem, but their larvae look like caterpillars and do similar damage. The yellow-and-black-blotched larvae of the glossy, blue-black berberis sawfly may completely strip a plant in a few weeks. This pest is a newcomer (arriving in 2002) and has not yet spread throughout the country.

PLANTS AFFECTED *Berberis thunbergii* and *B. vulgaris* are particularly susceptible; mahonias can also be attacked.

HOW BAD IS IT? The defoliation is unsightly and will reduce the vigour of the plant if not stopped.

PREVENTION AND CONTROL Check under the leaves regularly from spring onwards. Where a few larvae are found, remove and squash them. If necessary, spray with pyrethrum insecticide. As a last resort, use an approved chemical pesticide.

Box blight

Two types of blights attack box plants. *Cylindrocladium* produces brown or black spots that eventually cover the leaf surface. The leaf undersides may produce a white, webby growth. Stems and bark also develop black streaking and dieback. *Volutella* is not quite as serious. Leaves affected by this turn brown and have pink spores on their undersides. Stems die off in distinct areas.

PLANTS AFFECTED *Buxus sempervirens*, *B. s.* 'Suffruticosa', *B. microphylla* and *B. sinica* in particular, although other species may also be infected.

HOW BAD IS IT? Plants are rarely killed but they are very disfigured and damaged as they regrow and get knocked back. The shape of clipped plants is spoiled.

PREVENTION AND CONTROL Carefully remove and dispose of infected leaves and stems. Keep tools and clothing clean to prevent further infection. Clip in dry weather (with hand shears rather than powered trimmers). Try growing the more blight-resistant *B. microphylla* 'Faulkner'.

Box sucker

Box sucker is a harmless, aphid-like insect. Its nymphs suck the sap from young shoots and leaves in late spring, distorting growth so the leaves curve like tiny cabbages. White, waxy honeydew (*see* page 68) drips from where the young are clustered.

PLANTS AFFECTED Box (*Buxus*).

HOW BAD IS IT? It is disfiguring, but if the plants are being clipped, which is often the case with box, the damage can be removed. Smaller plants may be stunted.

PREVENTION AND CONTROL If you are worried about small plants, spray with an approved chemical insecticide as soon as you see the nymphs in spring, as the plant starts into growth. Spraying after the damage is done achieves nothing.

Capsid bug

From late spring to late summer, these pale green bugs feed on the sap of developing shoots, injecting toxic saliva that kills the plant cells. As the shoots grow, the dead cells leave tiny holes in the leaves, and the flowers are misshapen.

PLANTS AFFECTED Many including chrysanthemums, dahlias, forsythias, fuchsias, magnolias, roses and salvias.

HOW BAD IS IT? The holed leaves look unattractive, but the damage to the flowers is more noticeable. They tend to open unevenly or drop off before opening.

PREVENTION AND CONTROL Hard to spot, so hand-picking is difficult. In most cases the damage can be lived with, but as a last resort spray with an approved insecticide as soon as bugs are seen.

Box blight

Box sucker

Capsid bug

Cabbage white caterpillar

Mullein moth caterpillar

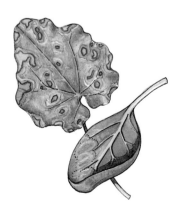

Downy mildew

Caterpillars

Most of us like to see butterflies and moths in the garden, so it is a pity their offspring can cause so much damage to our precious plants. Some caterpillars eat stems and roots (*see* pages 82 and 98), but their most common and obvious feeding sites are the leaves. Sawfly larvae (*see* page 65), which do similar damage, resemble caterpillars but have more legs – sawfly larvae usually have seven pairs, while caterpillars have between two and five pairs. (*See also* Leaf miners, page 69.)

PLANTS AFFECTED Many including birch (*Betula*), buddleia, cotoneaster, delphinium, euonymus, fuchsia, hawthorn (*Crataegus*), hazel (*Corylus*), monkshood (*Aconitum*), roses, sedum and water lilies (*see* page 75). Cabbage white caterpillars also attack ornamentals in the brassica family, and mullein moth can strip verbascums and figwort (*Scrophularia*).

HOW BAD IS IT? Mostly the effect is cosmetic, since plants recover and grow normally the following season. Successive attacks weaken plants.

PREVENTION AND CONTROL Pick off small infestations. Go hunting after dark too; many caterpillars feed at night. Some have fine hairs that can irritate the skin, eyes and mouth: remove these by pruning. Pheromone traps can be helpful for monitoring and identification. For larger numbers use pyrethrum spray or, as a last resort, an approved chemical insecticide.

Downy mildew

Downy mildew is common in wet seasons. The first signs are discoloured patches, usually yellowish, on the upper leaf surface, with floury, grey or purplish-white fungal growth on the underside. The infected area usually expands to cover the leaf. (Powdery mildew is similar, *see* page 70.)

PLANTS AFFECTED Many, but most vulnerable are young plants and seedlings that are growing in moist and poorly ventilated conditions.

HOW BAD IS IT? The fungus stunts growth and weakens plants, making them likely to succumb to other diseases, such as grey mould (*see* page 68). It can kill seedlings, and the variety that affects busy lizzies (*Impatiens*) is usually fatal.

PREVENTION AND CONTROL Avoid watering from above in greenhouses and improve air circulation around young plants, both in greenhouses and outdoors, so that the leaves will dry quickly when wet. There are no chemical cures. Remove affected leaves promptly, and do not compost parts, since the spores will survive.

Earwigs

Small, brown creatures with distinctive tail pincers, earwigs leave little round holes or notches in leaves and flower petals. They are more common inside greenhouses and cold frames, where the damage they cause is also less likely to be tolerated. On the plus side, they do eat aphids.

PLANTS AFFECTED Many, but most noticeably those with large flowers, such as carnations (*Dianthus*), chrysanthemums, clematis and dahlias.

HOW BAD IS IT? The damage is purely cosmetic and irritating; the plants will hardly notice it.

PREVENTION AND CONTROL Make a simple trap by filling a jam jar or plant pot with straw or shredded paper. Stick a cane into the soil and place the pot or jar upside down on top, among the tops of the plants. Adult earwigs find this an irresistible hidy-hole overnight. In the morning, before they are on the move again, simply empty the trap away from your plants or near an aphid-infested specimen.

Eelworms

Eelworms, or nematodes, are microscopic. There are many different types and we use some as biological controls (*see* page 27), but several can cause significant damage through feeding, either on leaves and stems or at the roots. Damage is usually worst in damp conditions in late summer and early autumn.

PLANTS AFFECTED Many including chrysanthemums, daffodils (*Narcissus*), penstemons and phlox; also shrubs. (*See also* Onion eelworm, page 95; Potato cyst eelworm, page 96; Root knot eelworm, page 113.)

HOW BAD IS IT? The foliage is marked or distorted and damaged and gradually dies. Flower production is affected. Plants eventually die.

PREVENTION AND CONTROL Destroy badly affected plants. It may be possible to save phlox by taking root cuttings. Cut daffodil bulbs in half to be sure eelworm is to blame: if there are brown concentric rings inside the bulb, dig up and burn all bulbs within 1m (40in) of affected bulbs.

Figwort weevil

The beetle-like figwort weevil has a white head with a distinctive snout and rough, blackish body. Both it and its slug-like, slimy larvae feed on leaves, buds and flowers from late spring to late summer. The larvae pupate in brown cocoons.

PLANTS AFFECTED Buddleia, figworts (*Scrophularia*), phygelius, verbascum.

HOW BAD IS IT? Affected parts dry up and die; eaten flower buds do not develop.

PREVENTION AND CONTROL Look out for the weevils in early spring when they emerge from hibernation to lay eggs. Pick them off and destroy them as well as the larvae and cocoons. As a last resort, spray with an approved chemical insecticide.

Flea beetles

Small, round holes scraped into the top leaf tissues but often not going the whole way through are typically made by flea beetles. These tiny, black, shiny beetles are active from mid-spring to late summer.

PLANTS AFFECTED Alyssum (*Lobularia*), aubrieta, fuchsias, nasturtiums (*Tropaeolum*), stocks (*Matthiola*) and wallflowers (both *Cheiranthus* and *Erysimum*). Radish, rocket, swedes, turnips and potatoes.

HOW BAD IS IT? A major attack will kill or seriously debilitate seedlings. Larger plants survive but will be disfigured and weaker.

PREVENTION AND CONTROL Ensure seedlings get off to a good start and grow fast to go beyond the point where damage is fatal. Sow seed when conditions are good. Spray with pyrethrum if necessary. As a last resort, use a suitable chemical insecticide.

Fungal wilts

A variety of different fungi, including *Fusarium* and *Verticillum* species, invade stems and leaves, causing wilting and eventually dieback. Sometimes staining can be seen in the tissues, often in streaks. Drought and waterlogging (*see* pages 17–18) are also common causes of wilt.

PLANTS AFFECTED Many woody, herbaceous and vegetable plants. (*See also* Clematis wilt, page 76; Damping off, page 81; Peony wilt, page 85.)

HOW BAD IS IT? Annuals and young plants die fairly quickly, while larger perennials, shrubs and trees may survive for a few years with stems and branches gradually dying off.

PREVENTION AND CONTROL Dig up and destroy badly affected plants. Do not replant in the same spot. If just a few stems or branches are affected, prune these out. Keep all tools clean to prevent the disease spreading. Grow resistant plants.

Eelworm

Flea beetle

Fungal wilt

Gall mites

These microscopic bugs feed on leaves and buds, secreting chemicals that cause distortion or galls (*see* page 62). These may show as thickened margins, curling, blistering, pin-like protrusions or hairy patches, often in red or purple. The affected buds usually fail to develop.

PLANTS AFFECTED Many including broom (*Cytisus*), crab apple (*Malus*), elm (*Ulmus*), fuchsia, maple (*Acer*), mountain ash (*Sorbus*) and grape vines (*Vitis*). (*See also* Blackcurrant big bud mite and gall midge, page 91; Pear leaf blister mite, page 95; Rose galls, page 87.)

HOW BAD IS IT? Although the symptoms are often unattractive, most gall mites do little real harm to plants. An exception is the recently arrived fuchsia gall mite (*Aculops fuchsiae*), which can halt new growth.

PREVENTION AND CONTROL On smaller shrubs or trees, where the galls are unsightly and few in number, affected buds or leaves can be picked off. It is obviously not sensible to remove large amounts of foliage. Infected fuchsias are notifiable and need to be destroyed.

Fuchsia gall mite

Grey mould (botrytis)

The fungus *Botrytis cinerea* invades plants through damaged tissues, causing yellowing, browning or spotting and then producing whitish or grey felt on leaves, fruit, flowers and stems. It grows anywhere on dead and living plant materials and flourishes in cool, damp conditions with poor air circulation.

PLANTS AFFECTED Almost any plant.

HOW BAD IS IT? It is disfiguring and can destroy large areas of the plants, especially those with soft stems.

PREVENTION AND CONTROL Keep plants growing healthily and make sure air circulation is good. Remove damaged and

Grey mould (botrytis)

infected stems to reduce the risk of infection. Tidy up plant debris to prevent the spores overwintering. Fungicides may help to prevent infection, but they are usually ineffective once the fungus has entered the plant and become visible.

Hellebore black death

Hellebore black death is thought to be a virus, which may invade plants via an aphid attack. Symptoms become obvious in mid-spring. The leaves are covered with black streaks and net-like patterning, and stems and flowers may also be affected.

PLANTS AFFECTED *Helleborus × hybridus* (syn. *H. orientalis*); other species may also show symptoms.

HOW BAD IS IT? It is fatal; remove affected plants as soon as possible.

PREVENTION AND CONTROL The infection can be dormant in plants for up to a year, so be careful when you buy new stock. Seed does not carry the virus. Once a plant is showing symptoms there is nothing that can be done. Dig it up and destroy it.

Honeydew and sooty mould

Honeydew is the sticky excrement of sap-sucking insects such as aphids (*see* page 64) and scale insects (*see* page 72). As they feed on leaf undersides, the honeydew drips onto the leaves below. It can encourage black sooty moulds. Ants may eat it and can be a nuisance, particularly in potted plants.

PLANTS AFFECTED Any plant that harbours sap-sucking insects.

HOW BAD IS IT? It can be the first indicator that your plant has a pest problem, so take a closer look. It can be irritating and is unsightly, but does not harm the plant.

PREVENTION AND CONTROL Treatment of the cause, such as aphids or other insects,

Hellebore black death

is the best way to avoid honeydew. If it is on smooth leaves, such as citrus, it can be washed off with a soapy solution.

Leafhoppers

Pale yellow with grey markings, leafhoppers are jumping and sap-sucking insects. Their creamy larvae are less mobile. They are common in greenhouses, but can breed year-round outdoors too. Signs of their presence include pale mottling of leaves.
PLANTS AFFECTED Many including foxgloves (*Digitalis*), primulas, rhododendrons, roses and salvias, as well as indoor plants and fruit.
HOW BAD IS IT? Most cause only minor damage, though the eaten leaves are unsightly. Some, such as rhododendron leafhopper, can introduce other problems (*see* Rhododendron bud blast, page 85).
PREVENTION AND CONTROL Use the biological control (*see* page 27) *Anagrus atomus* in greenhouses. Use fatty acids, plant oils or pyrethrum. As a last resort, use an approved chemical insecticide. Several applications may be needed. Spray in early to mid-spring before any infestations become severe.

Leaf miners

Pale blotches or lines visible inside the leaf tissues are usually made by the larvae of beetles, flies, moths or sawflies. Often the larvae can be seen inside their 'mine' by holding the leaf up to the light.
PLANTS AFFECTED There are numerous leaf miners, many with specific hosts, such as alliums, chrysanthemums, horse chestnut (*see* page 63) and sempervivums.
HOW BAD IS IT? Heavy infestations are disfiguring, but they are never fatal.
PREVENTION AND CONTROL Small infestations of leaf miners can be squashed

while inside the leaves, or badly damaged leaves can be removed. Because they live within the leaf tissues, leaf miners are difficult to control with pesticides.

Leaf spots

Bacterial leaf spots are circular or less distinct shapes, often surrounded by paler or yellow tissue. Fungal spots are brown or grey and first appear as patches that may spread to cover the leaf. Closer inspection usually reveals tiny, black or brown pimples, which are the fruiting bodies.
PLANTS AFFECTED Almost all plants. Fungal species often have specific hosts including hydrangeas, ivies (*Hedera*), pansies (*Viola*) and rhododendrons.
HOW BAD IS IT? Spots are unattractive but not usually very debilitating. If plants falter, check for underlying problems.
PREVENTION AND CONTROL Pick off infected leaves. Gather and destroy debris in the autumn and mulch to prevent spores reinfecting the plants. As a last resort, use a fungicide as a preventative measure – but this will not work on all fungal leaf spots.

Leaf weevils

Weevils eat ragged holes along the edges of leaves. These beetle-like creatures are usually bright blue-green or brassy brown and can sometimes be very numerous. Vine weevils (*see* page 83) are more serious because they also damage roots.
PLANTS AFFECTED Deciduous plants, especially apples (*Malus*), birches (*Betula*), cherries (*Prunus*) and rowans (*Sorbus*).
HOW BAD IS IT? Damage is unattractive, but will not harm the tree.
PREVENTION AND CONTROL It is best to tolerate leaf weevils. Where small trees are infested, spray with an approved chemical insecticide as a last resort.

Honeydew and sooty mould

Leaf miner

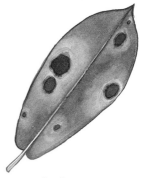

Leaf spot

Lily beetle

The red-shelled lily beetle is a foreign pest. It looks lovely but has dreadful habits, and its young are even worse. They cover their fat little bodies with excrement, so when you see them on the undersides of the leaves it is easy to dismiss them as plant debris. Both adults and young cause extensive damage from early spring until late summer.

PLANTS AFFECTED Lilies (*Lilium*) and fritillaries (*Fritillaria*).

HOW BAD IS IT? Plants are not killed but they are so badly damaged that they are no longer ornamental.

PREVENTION AND CONTROL Pick or shake off the grubs (wear gloves if you are squeamish). Pick off the adults. They are very good at dropping off the plants and making themselves invisible by lying on their backs, so put a cloth on the ground first so that you can see them. As a last resort, spray the larvae with an approved chemical pesticide.

Mealy bug

From a distance, mealy bugs look a bit like tufts of white cotton stuck in leaf junctions and other tight spots, but they are more like white woodlice with long feelers when seen close up. The white, waxy fluff that they cover themselves in conceals their eggs, too. Like many insect pests they excrete honeydew (*see* page 68) as part of their feeding activities.

PLANTS AFFECTED This tends to be an indoor pest, infesting plants in the conservatory, greenhouse and house. Cacti are particularly vulnerable.

HOW BAD IS IT? Mealy bugs are conspicuous and unattractive and will debilitate the plant. Their honeydew encourages the growth of black sooty moulds (*see* page 68).

PREVENTION AND CONTROL In greenhouses and conservatories, the ladybird biological control *Cryptolaemus montrouzieri* can be used (*see* page 27). On plants with few leaves, such as small rubber plants (*Ficus*), the bugs can be washed off when seen. Otherwise, use a spray containing fatty acids or plant oils. As a last resort, spray with an approved chemical pesticide.

Powdery mildew

This fungal disease appears as a whitish powder covering the upper surfaces of the leaves. The foliage turns yellow and becomes thin-textured. Young leaves are usually more badly affected and may become misshapen. The disease often spreads to stems and fruit. (Downy mildew is similar, *see* page 66.)

PLANTS AFFECTED Most including clematis, gooseberries (*see* American gooseberry mildew, page 90), honeysuckle (*Lonicera*), pansies (*Viola*), phlox and roses (*see* page 88).

HOW BAD IS IT? Annual plants and youngsters are most badly affected. Fruit may split and spoil. Many annuals, such as pot marigolds (*Calendula*), cucumbers and peas, suffer from powdery mildew towards the end of their life, when it is not a cause for concern.

PREVENTION AND CONTROL The main cause of powdery mildew is a combination of dry roots and damp leaves. Keep your plants well watered, but avoid watering from above and wetting the leaves. Use mulches (*see* page 33) where possible. Reduce overcrowding and increase air circulation, and clear away debris to prevent spores overwintering. Where only a few leaves on a plant are affected they can be removed and burned. As a last resort, use a fungicide.

Lily beetle

Mealy bug

Powdery mildew

Red spider mite

Red spider mites are microscopic, but they create a visible, fine web on the underside of leaves. As the mite feeds on them, leaves become yellow and may curl up and look pitted and dry. Spider mites are more common in dry conditions such as in a greenhouse, against a sunny wall outdoors or on plants growing indoors.

PLANTS AFFECTED Very common and widespread on a huge range of plants.

HOW BAD IS IT? It is debilitating and disfiguring. A bad or prolonged attack stunts growth but rarely kills plants.

PREVENTION AND CONTROL Increase humidity by spraying the plant with water once or twice daily, particularly the leaf undersides. Stand potted plants on gravel-filled trays full of water. In a greenhouse, use the biological control *Phytoseiulus persimilis* (*see* page 27). Spray with plant oils or fatty acids. As a last resort, use an approved chemical pesticide.

Rhododendron lacebug

The rhododendron lacebug, *Stephanitis rhododendri*, has a shiny, black-brown body and lacy wings. Adults and nymphs feed on leaf undersides, turning leaves mottled green and making the edges curl under. The undersides are marked with rusty brown excrement. They thrive on plants in sunny sites and during dry weather.

PLANTS AFFECTED Rhododendrons. Some varieties are resistant. Pieris are attacked by a related pest.

HOW BAD IS IT? Disfiguring; a heavy infestation can be very debilitating.

PREVENTION AND CONTROL Plant rhododendrons and azaleas in a shady site. Spray with pyrethrum, particularly towards the end of summer to prevent the adults laying eggs. As a last resort, use an approved chemical pesticide.

Rosemary leaf beetle

The rosemary beetle is dark metallic green with red-purple stripes. Both it and its young feed on foliage, mostly in late summer and autumn. Although a relative newcomer to Britain (arriving in the 1990s), it is already very widespread.

PLANTS AFFECTED Rosemary, lavender, Russian sage (*Perovskia*) and thyme.

HOW BAD IS IT? Not a huge problem if numbers are kept down.

PREVENTION AND CONTROL Pick the beetles off plants by hand, or place a cloth under the plant and give it a shake to dislodge them. Spray the larvae with pyrethrum if necessary, in spring or late summer to early autumn. As a last resort, use an approved pesticide.

Rusts

Rusts are signs of fungal infection and are common and widespread, particularly in damp conditions or where air does not circulate freely. Leaves become speckled with orange, red-brown or yellow spots – clusters of fungal spores – sometimes spreading over the entire surface. Affected foliage may discolour and die.

PLANTS AFFECTED Anemones, snapdragons (*Antirrhinum*), flowering cherries (*Prunus*), fuchsias, hollyhocks (*Alcea*), irises, periwinkles (*Vinca*), rhododendrons, roses (*see* page 89), as well as fruit and vegetables (*see* page 96).

HOW BAD IS IT? Rust is disfiguring and often very debilitating. Plants may be so badly affected that they have to be disposed of to prevent further spread of the infection.

PREVENTION AND CONTROL Remove affected parts and destroy them. Increase air circulation around plants and grow resistant varieties where possible. As a last resort, use a fungicide.

Red spider mite

Rhododendron lacebug

Rosemary leaf beetle

Scale insect

Shot-hole disease

Sawflies

Sawflies are very common and cause few problems as adults. However, their larvae, which look somewhat like caterpillars, have a voracious appetite, usually for leaves, but some attack fruit.

PLANTS AFFECTED Columbine (*Aquilegia*), goat's beard (*Aruncus*), geranium, geum, Solomon's seal (*Polygonatum*). (*See also* Leaf miners, page 69; Slugworms, pages 89 and 97.)

HOW BAD IS IT? Defoliation can be almost total. Although plants are unlikely to die, they will be severely disfigured and may be less vigorous in subsequent years.

PREVENTION AND CONTROL Picking off the larvae is fiddly, but may be worth doing with small infestations. Spray with pyrethrum. As a last resort, use an approved chemical pesticide.

Scale insects

Scale insects are flat, limpet-like creatures, usually in shades of brown. They cling to leaves and stems and excrete honeydew, which encourages black sooty mould (*see* page 68). Some species lay eggs in a conspicuous white mass.

PLANTS AFFECTED Many including hydrangea, juniper and wisteria; potted citrus and bay (*Laurus*) trees.

HOW BAD IS IT? Heavy attacks can cause yellowing of the foliage and reduce vigour, but usually the honeydew is the most annoying factor.

PREVENTION AND CONTROL Rub the scales from smaller plants with your fingers or a cotton bud soaked in diluted washing-up liquid or soft soap. Larger plants shrug off attacks without much of a problem. Under cover use the parasitic wasp *Metaphycus helvolus* (*see* page 27). As a last resort, use an approved chemical pesticide. This is most effective in midsummer, when the young nymphs are vulnerable. Scale insects breed continuously under cover, so extend spraying periods.

Shot-hole disease

This fungal disease is more common in plants that are struggling. Young foliage develops small, brown spots that grow with the expanding leaves. The damaged tissue eventually falls out, leaving holes.

PLANTS AFFECTED Members of the cherry family (*Prunus*), including ornamental cherries, laurel and fruit trees.

HOW BAD IS IT? Disfiguring but not usually fatal, so long as the causes are dealt with. (*See also* Cankers, page 76; Powdery mildew, page 70.)

PREVENTION AND CONTROL Water well during dry spells and feed and mulch when necessary (*see* page 33). As a last resort, spray with Bordeaux mixture (an organic mixture of copper sulphate and hydrated lime used as a fungicide) as the leaves emerge and at leaf fall.

Smuts

These fungal diseases produce swollen areas on the leaves, flowers or stems that burst to release black spores.

PLANTS AFFECTED Anemones, dahlias, pinks (*Dianthus*), trollius, violets, winter aconites (*Eranthis*), and leeks and onions.

HOW BAD IS IT? Flowers may be spoiled. The disease is usually restricted to the area with the symptoms, but smuts in pinks and winter aconites spread through the plant, which should be destroyed.

PREVENTION AND CONTROL Pick off infected areas before the spores burst out. Clear away dead plant material in autumn. Destroy any affected vegetable plants and don't grow members of the onion family in the same spot for at least five years.

Smut

Snails and slugs

Of all the pests in the garden, slugs and snails are among the worst. They do a great deal of damage in a short space of time, attacking plants year-round, except when temperatures drop to below 5°C (40°F). Some slugs live permanently underground, eating roots and bulbs.

PLANTS AFFECTED Many. Among the most badly damaged are dahlias, hostas, lettuces, lupins and delphiniums, and seedlings of any plants are vulnerable.

HOW BAD IS IT? Damage ranges from disfigurement to death.

PREVENTION AND CONTROL Nothing will entirely rid you of these pests, so aim to protect your most precious plants and reduce numbers. In small areas, use the biological control *Phasmarhabditis hermaphrodita* (*see* page 27), but this is unlikely to affect snails. Collect slugs and snails in a bucket after dark on damp nights. You have to kill them, though; if you chuck them over the hedge they will return. Barriers are most suitable for potted plants or in raised beds. Grit can be used around plants (*see* page 117), as can copper collars (*see* page 26), which are thought to give them a small electric shock. Slug pellets are widely used. Aluminium sulphate is reasonably environmentally friendly; ferric phosphate is more effective. If you must use metaldehyde pellets, use them in tiny quantities. Sprinkle them under upturned flowerpots or lengths of guttering so that birds and your pets cannot get at them. Clear away dead slugs on a daily basis.

Tarsonemid mites

These miniscule sap-sucking insects are mostly pests of indoor and greenhouse plants. They feed on developing leaves and flowers, causing stunting and distortion, brown or white flecking on petals and sometimes brown marking on stems.

PLANTS AFFECTED Many indoor plants including African violets (*Saintpaulia*), begonias, busy lizzies (*Impatiens*), cyclamen, gloxinias and pelargoniums. Some garden plants, notably Michaelmas daisies (*Aster novi-belgii*) and strawberries.

HOW BAD IS IT? The damage is unattractive, and a heavy infestation can stop the shoots from growing.

PREVENTION AND CONTROL Although picking off the developing shoots is sometimes advocated as a control, this has obvious disadvantages. Plants are best destroyed to prevent other specimens becoming infected.

Thrips

Thrips are tiny, narrowish sap-sucking insects, often black. Their feeding produces silvery spotting and patching over the upper leaf surfaces, accompanied by brown or black staining from the thrips' excreta. Hot weather increases numbers and heavy infestations may prevent flowers from developing.

PLANTS AFFECTED Many including gladiolus, privet (*Ligustrum*) and *Viburnum tinus* outdoors and busy lizzies (*Impatiens*), cyclamen, fuchsias, gloxinias and rubber and cheese plants (*Ficus* and *Monstera*) under cover. Also vegetables, notably leeks and onions and pea pods (*see* page 102).

HOW BAD IS IT? Where plants are grown for their foliage, such as house plants, the damage is very unsightly. Flowering plants may not flower. Thrips can spread viruses.

PREVENTION AND CONTROL In greenhouses use the biological control *Amblyseius degenerans*. Pyrethrum sprays can be used elsewhere. As a last resort, use an approved chemical pesticide. Several applications may be needed.

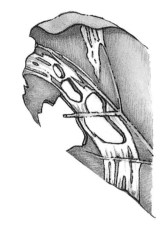

Snail and slug

Thrips

Tulip fire

This is a fungal disease of tulips that affects all parts and ruins the flowers. The emerging leaves have pale brown flecking over their surfaces and may also be distorted. They soon develop a grey fungal growth. If the flowers open, the petals may be marked with pale spots, but often flower buds do not open or even appear.

PLANTS AFFECTED Tulips.

HOW BAD IS IT? Plants affected will never recover and must be destroyed to prevent spread.

PREVENTION AND CONTROL Once tulips show signs of infection they must be dug up and destroyed. Do not grow them in the same place for at least three years. To avoid the problem, change your tulip beds every two years. Buy bulbs from a reputable source.

Viruses

Yellow streaks, spots or angular patches, mottling and other oddities in the leaf colouring are most likely to be caused by viruses. Affected plants are usually also stunted and distorted, sometimes without leaf colouring being affected. Plants will perform badly, not developing flower buds or fruit, for example. Where flowers do open their colouring may be streaked or mottled. Orchid viruses may show as dark brown or black mottling.

PLANTS AFFECTED Many including daffodils (*Narcissus*), dahlias, delphiniums, freesias, gladioli, lilies, lupins, orchids, pelargoniums, petunias, roses (*see* page 89) and sweet peas (*Lathyrus*). Also vegetables (*see* page 97).

HOW BAD IS IT? Plants do not recover from virus attacks, so should be destroyed.

PREVENTION AND CONTROL Aphids and other sap-sucking insects spread viruses, so control these. Weeds may harbour viruses while looking healthy, so keep on top of your weeding. Fungi and soil organisms may also carry viruses, but there is little you can do about them. Keep all your tools clean, since pruning and trimming can spread viruses between plants. Some plants are virus resistant, others are grown from virus-free stock, so choose these wherever possible. Where you have lost plants to viruses do not replant similar varieties in the same place.

Whitefly

Whitefly infestation is easily diagnosed: when you tap or brush past an infested plant, these dandruff-like flies depart *en masse* from under the leaves. Like many other sap-suckers, they excrete honeydew (*see* page 68). Their nymphs also suck sap and can be found on the leaf undersides: they look like tiny scales.

PLANTS AFFECTED Many greenhouse plants including vegetables like tomatoes and cucumbers. Outdoors, honeysuckle (*Lonicera*), rhododendrons, strawberry trees (*Arbutus*) and *Viburnum tinus*.

HOW BAD IS IT? The unattractive sooty mould that grows on the honeydew is the worst aspect of most whitefly attacks, though heavy infestations in greenhouses can be debilitating.

PREVENTION AND CONTROL Use the biological control *Encarsia formosa* (*see* page 27) in greenhouses. Some whitefly are resistant to pyrethrum: use fatty acid sprays or plant oils, or as a last resort an approved chemical pesticide.

See also

Clematis wilt (page 76), Cuckoo spit (page 77), Damping off (page 81), Dieback (page 78), Fasciation (page 78), Silver leaf disease (page 97), Slugworms (page 97).

Viruses

Whitefly

Pond problems

Algae

Particular weather conditions – hot, sunny and dry – encourage algal growth, which can spread very quickly. Blanket weed has soft, silky growth that spreads across the water. It is easily removed with a cane or broom handle. Scummy growths may also occur. Looking like green, curdled milk, they dissolve when you try to touch them.

PLANTS AFFECTED Algae are not harmful to plants.

HOW BAD IS IT? Apart from looking ugly, heavy crops deoxygenate the water.

PREVENTION AND CONTROL Lack of shade is the main cause of algal growth; add pond plants to cover more of the water's surface. Sludge can also promote it, since algae thrive on excess nutrients found in rotting plant matter. Try to prevent leaves falling into the pond, and remove a proportion of the sludge each year. Leave it on the side for 24 hours or so for any pond life to return to the water. Barley straw stuffed into mesh bags or products containing barley straw extracts, available from garden centres, may help. Fountains help to aerate the water and prevent algae building up.

China mark caterpillar

The china mark moth is brown with heavy white squiggles and blotches. It lives in plants around pond edges and lays eggs on floating leaves. When the caterpillars hatch, they remove a small section of leaf to make cocoons on the leaf undersides. They feed on a range of pond plants including duckweed.

PLANTS AFFECTED Water lilies and other pond plants with floating leaves, such as curled pondweed (*Potamogeton*).

HOW BAD IS IT? Damage is cosmetic.

PREVENTION AND CONTROL Check under the leaves of water lilies and other water plants and pick off the protective cocoons. Never use insecticides near water.

Chironomid midges

The larvae of these midges graze around the edges of floating pond plants, giving them a ragged appearance. The damaged leaves turn yellow and die, rotting away. The larvae may be red (called bloodworms) or transparent, while the midges, which are non-biting, usually have long, slender bodies and long legs.

PLANTS AFFECTED Pond plants including curled pondweed (*Potamogeton*), frog-bit (*Hydrocharis*) and water lilies.

HOW BAD IS IT? Unsightly and initially debilitating, but usually short term.

PREVENTION AND CONTROL New ponds soon become home to a range of insects and other organisms that keep the midge larvae under control. There are no chemical controls safe for use near water.

Water lily beetle

Long, narrow and wiggly holes cut into water lily pads are made by the water lily beetle. Rich yellowy brown with darker markings, the beetles start feeding in late spring. Their larvae hatch out by midsummer and also eat the leaves. Later the adults will eat the flowers too.

PLANTS AFFECTED Water lilies.

HOW BAD IS IT? Beautiful plants become an eyesore. Extensive damage makes the pads rot, so plant vigour is affected.

PREVENTION AND CONTROL On smaller ponds, pick off larvae or blast them off with a hosepipe. There are no chemical controls that are safe for use near water.

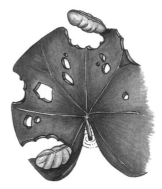

China mark caterpillar

Chironomid midge

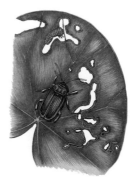

Water lily beetle

Stem and bark problems

Bark beetle

Cytospora canker

Nectria canker

Bark beetles

There are many different species of bark beetle. Adult beetles tunnel into wood where they lay their eggs and the larvae then tunnel out again, emerging as adults. They prefer dead wood, so they are most likely to be found on damaged or dying branches. (*See also* Dutch elm disease, page 78; Shot-hole borer, page 80.)
PLANTS AFFECTED Woody plants.
HOW BAD IS IT? The beetles can allow disease to get into the plant, or they may indicate it is already in poor health.
PREVENTION AND CONTROL Prune out any dead, dying, damaged or diseased wood. Check the tree or shrub for other signs of underlying disease, such as fungus (*see* pages 78–9).

Beech bark disease

When plants are infected with this disease, patches of bark die off, allowing sap to escape as a black, sticky gum. The affected areas appear to sink into the bark. They grow bigger, and small fruiting bodies like red pimples appear. Leaves in subsequent years will be smaller than usual and yellow-green. The disease seems to be associated with beech bark scale, a minuscule insect that covers itself in a conspicuous white powder, which can be seen in cracks in the bark.
PLANTS AFFECTED Beech (*Fagus*) trees. Saplings are less likely to be affected than mature trees.
HOW BAD IS IT? Trees must usually be felled, since the disease makes them likely to shed branches and eventually die.
PREVENTION AND CONTROL Though apparently harmless, beech bark scale insects may allow the fungus into the bark. There is no remedy.

Cankers

Cankers can be caused by bacterial or fungal infections and are characterized by the death of patches of bark and, in many cases, oozing of sap or other substances from the area. Cankered bark is usually discoloured and rough-textured, splitting around and through the affected area. It can be raised above the rest of the bark, or sunken. Once the cankered area girdles a branch or stem, the growth above it will be affected. Leaves may be smaller, distorted and yellowing, while flowers and fruit may be aborted. Eventually, the limb will die. Apple canker often follows attacks by woolly aphids.
PLANTS AFFECTED Many including members of the apple (*Malus*) and cherry (*Prunus*) families, mulberries (*Morus*), pears (*Pyrus*), rowans (*Sorbus*), roses (*see* page 87), willows (*Salix*) and several conifers.
HOW BAD IS IT? In many cases, canker may be controlled if caught early enough, but once it has spread through the plant there is no cure.
PREVENTION AND CONTROL Act as soon as you spot lesions. Look out for yellowing leaves on conifers, because cankers are disguised on their rough bark. Remove affected branches, making sure that you cut well below the diseased area. Clean your pruning tools between cuts, so as not to reinfect as you prune. Improve drainage and general growing conditions.

Clematis wilt

Clematis wilt is very frustrating, since it can strike at any time and its effect is almost instantaneous. For example, a long stem of buds, ready to burst into abundant flower, first droops, then withers and dies in a matter of days. Alternatively, a newly

planted clematis never emerges, or if it does it keeps dying back and eventually gives up trying. The cause is a fungus that invades the stems, blocking the tissues that conduct water around the plant.
PLANTS AFFECTED Mostly large-flowered cultivars; species and small-flowered cultivars are more resistant.
HOW BAD IS IT? It ranges from being the cause of great disappointment to being fatal.
PREVENTION AND CONTROL Remove affected stems down to healthy buds, which often means cutting below the soil surface. New shoots should arise. When planting new clematis, position the rootball so that the top of the potting compost from the pot is below the soil surface in the garden, but no deeper than 8cm (3in); this encourages lots of new growth buds, at least some of which should be disease-free.

Coral spot

This fungal disease appears as pink or red-orange (coral-coloured) spots on the bark of dead stems of woody plants. The fungus, which also lives in woody debris, enters plants through damaged bark and pruning wounds. It causes dieback and may spread through the whole plant.
PLANTS AFFECTED Many different plants, but currants (*Ribes*), elaeagnus, magnolias, maples (*Acer*), pyracanthas and wisterias are particularly susceptible.
HOW BAD IS IT? This fungus is disfiguring and can kill.
PREVENTION AND CONTROL Prune out all infected wood and any that shows signs of dieback. Cut back into healthy tissue. Keep all tools clean as you work. Burn or otherwise dispose of the infected material. Always prune to just above a leaf-joint; snags can cause dieback.

Crown gall

Caused by bacterial infection, these galls usually appear at the base of plants but may also grow further up the trunk or stems. They form hard, rounded, corky growths that are white at first but mature to brown, and can grow to well over 30cm (12in) on tree trunks. They remain indefinitely on woody plants but soften and burst on herbaceous ones.
PLANTS AFFECTED Many including fruits, vegetables, perennials, shrubs and trees.
HOW BAD IS IT? Plants often seem unaffected, although their vigour might be reduced, especially where the galls encircle the main stem or trunk.
PREVENTION AND CONTROL Dig up and destroy infected plants to prevent spread. The bacteria enter via wounds, so avoid damage, including pruning, if plants in your garden have suffered from crown gall in the past. In vegetable gardens, grow potatoes in infected areas since they are not prone to crown gall.

Cuckoo spit

Cuckoo spit is a protective foam that covers the larvae of the froghopper. These nymphs are pale yellow-green and they feed on the sap of the plant; as they mature into adults the 'spit' disappears.
PLANTS AFFECTED Many, mostly herbaceous perennials, particularly wallflowers (*Cheiranthus* and *Erysimum*), and many wildflowers.
HOW BAD IS IT? Despite the rather conspicuous appearance of the foam, the nymphs rarely do any harm and the problem is only temporary.
PREVENTION AND CONTROL If you are worried about precious plants, pick off the nymphs by hand; otherwise, let nature take her course.

Coral spot

Crown gall

Cuckoo spit

Dieback

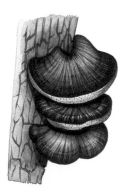

Fasciation

Fistulina fungal bracket

Dieback

Where parts of plants start to die off, often from the tips of the shoots downwards, but also from the base of the plant upwards, this is known as dieback. It is caused by fungal diseases that usually gain entry into the plant via tissue that has been damaged, for example by clumsy pruning. Poor planting and difficult growing conditions can also cause dieback.

PLANTS AFFECTED All.

HOW BAD IS IT? At best unattractive and disfiguring, at worst it can kill.

PREVENTION AND CONTROL Where woody stems are affected, prune them out well below the dead area. Make clean cuts just above a bud, because short stubs of stem with no buds on them are prone to dieback. If the plant is struggling, either move it somewhere more suitable or improve its growing conditions (*see* pages 14–18).

Dutch elm disease

This is not a Dutch disease; it was simply Dutch scientists who discovered what was causing it. There are two parts to the problem. Bark beetles (*see* page 76) feed under the bark and tunnel into the wood. They introduce the disease fungus *Ophiostoma novo-ulmi*. First the leaves wilt, then twigs and smaller branches die back and bark falls off in long strips. Even large trees can be killed very quickly.

PLANTS AFFECTED Many species of elm (*Ulmus*) and *Zelkova*.

HOW BAD IS IT? It is serious and eventually fatal. Dutch elm disease has killed over 25 million trees in Britain in the last 100 years.

PREVENTION AND CONTROL There are no chemical controls. Attempts are being made to breed resistant trees, with some success. Small specimens and those kept trimmed seem to be less attractive to the infecting beetle; species from Asia, where the disease is thought to have originated, show resistance.

Fasciation

Fasciation is a distortion of the shoot or flower stem, which grows very much wider than usual but is also almost completely flat, somewhat like a ribbon. Buds or leaves on the stem are usually normal, although flattened flowers are sometimes produced. Often only one or two shoots are affected and the rest of the plant is normal.

PLANTS AFFECTED Almost any.

HOW BAD IS IT? It is just an oddity and causes no harm at all.

PREVENTION AND CONTROL Very early damage to the growing-tips is thought to be a major cause of fasciation. It could be slugs or other pests feeding, cold weather at the wrong moment or even just a gardener brushing past. Viral diseases are another possible cause. This is a rare condition and seldom occurs more than once on the same plant. Remove the offending stem if necessary.

Fungal brackets

Any fungus usually has two distinct parts: a root-like mycelium in the soil or within the host plant, and fruiting bodies, which contain spores. Some are benign, but when harmful fungi invade plants, the mycelia spread via the vascular tissue, which is the equivalent of the plant's bloodstream, blocking its flow and causing wilting and dieback (*see* above). Under suitable conditions, the fruiting bodies appear on the plant's outer surfaces. They range from tiny pimples and dots to shelf-like 'brackets'. In brackets the spores are carried on the underside and float out like fine dust when they are ripe, sometimes staining the bark beneath.

PLANTS AFFECTED Any woody plants, but most commonly older trees and larger shrubs.

HOW BAD IS IT? When brackets form, you can be pretty sure that the tree's whole internal system is badly infected with fungal disease. Branches may split and break off or drop with very little warning. It is important to have the tree assessed by an arboriculturist for safety, and it will often need felling.

PREVENTION AND CONTROL Fungal diseases often enter plants through damaged bark caused by bark beetles (see page 76) or poor pruning techniques, wind damage and so on. Once they are inside, their spread cannot be prevented, but removing the brackets will reduce spore numbers. Healthy plants that are growing in suitable conditions are less likely to succumb to such diseases.

Honey fungus

This very destructive fungal disease produces honey-brown 'mushrooms' in autumn. However, infected trees or shrubs will already be looking unwell, perhaps dying back in patches, or maybe flowering better than usual in a last-ditch attempt to set seed. Digging at the plant base releases a mushroomy smell and may unearth thick, root-like fungal 'bootlaces'. A sheet of white fungal growth or black bootlaces under the bark confirm infection.

PLANTS AFFECTED Many, but some are particularly susceptible, including birches (*Betula*), buddleia, ceanothus, Leyland cypress (× *Cuprocyparis leylandii*), lilac

(*Syringa*), privet (*Ligustrum*), members of the *Prunus* family, roses and viburnum.

HOW BAD IS IT? Once they are infected, plants will die. They should be removed as soon as possible to prevent spread of the infection.

PREVENTION AND CONTROL Barriers of thick plastic sheeting or pond lining buried to a depth of 45cm (18in) may be used to protect healthy plants, but the fungus spreads far and wide so you may be too late. Regular deep digging (see page 20) will disturb the soil and break up the strands. Some plants are resistant, including box (*Buxus sempervirens*), clematis, hornbeam (*Carpinus betulus*), pittosporum and lime (*Tilia*).

Sclerotinia rot

Black, pellet-like sclerotia (dormant fruiting bodies) and white, fluffy fungal growth on stems and fruit are symptoms of infection with sclerotinia rot. The affected plants will suddenly collapse and die, and their infected tissues will start to rot, turning brown. Sclerotinia can also infect stored bulbs and tubers, in which it will produce a dry rot.

PLANTS AFFECTED Many, including chrysanthemums, dahlias, delphiniums, gladiolus and sunflowers (*Helianthus*), as well as stored bulbs and corms, growing cucumbers and stored root vegetables such as carrots and parsnips.

HOW BAD IS IT? The disease moves very quickly and soon kills affected plants. Stored vegetables will be inedible.

PREVENTION AND CONTROL Destroy all infected plant material to prevent the spread of the fungus and clear away debris. Do not grow vulnerable plants in the same site for at least four years; spores will overwinter in the soil to infect new plants in the spring.

Laetiporus fungal bracket

Honey fungus

Sclerotinia rot

Shot-hole borer

Shot-hole borers are a type of bark beetle (*see* page 76) that make distinctive round holes in tree bark. Beneath the bark, usually on branches, the tree is riddled with tunnels that each contain a feeding grub. Some species burrow deep into the tree, others make more superficial holes.

PLANTS AFFECTED Pears and apples, and members of the *Prunus* family, including cherries and plums.

HOW BAD IS IT? The presence of beetles is a sign your trees are unhappy, rather than the cause of problems.

PREVENTION AND CONTROL Make sure the trees have the growing conditions they need, in particular good drainage and adequate food and water. Remove any branches that are showing signs of infestation or dying back.

Squirrels

If you are visited by the small, red-brown, tufted-eared variety of squirrel, you have cause to rejoice. However, most of us are more likely to see grey squirrels – bigger, bolder and bordering on being vandals. They dig up corms and bulbs, eat flower buds and shoots, steal fruit and nuts and strip bark from branches.

PLANTS AFFECTED Crocus, tulips, nut and fruit plants, including strawberries. Bark from ash (*Fraxinus*), beech (*Fagus*) and sycamore (*Acer campestre*) is popular, as are buds of camellias and magnolias.

HOW BAD IS IT? The damage can be extensive and irritating; stripped bark can let disease into branches, causing dieback.

PREVENTION AND CONTROL Barriers, such as fruit cages, prevent damage to certain plants, but these must be sturdy; squirrels can chew through plastic and thinner wire meshes. The presence of dogs or cats can be a deterrent. Trapping may be temporarily successful, but you have to dispose of the trapped animal, and other squirrels will soon take its place.

Sudden oak death

The fungus *Phytophthora ramorum* causes this disease, which got its startling name because of the havoc it wreaked in American oaks. It gains entry at the trunk base and spreads quickly. Symptoms vary, but leaves may develop brown marks, often V-shaped; discoloration also appears on the stems and shoots. Bleeding cankers (*see* page 76) ooze brown or black liquid, and there is red or brown rotting under the bark.

PLANTS AFFECTED Camellias, rhododendrons (particularly *R. ponticum*) and viburnums. Also beech (*Fagus*), pieris, *Kalmia*, *Leucothoe*, larch (*Larix*) and some oaks (*Quercus*).

HOW BAD IS IT? Harmful. Affected plants must be destroyed.

PREVENTION AND CONTROL Be vigilant and report this notifiable disease if you see it anywhere. Cases must be dealt with by local authorities.

Witches' brooms

Unnaturally dense clumps of small stems and twigs on branches are known as witches' brooms. These are thought to be caused by fungal infections, although mite infestations may also be a factor.

PLANTS AFFECTED Birches (*Betula*) and a range of trees including hornbeams (*Carpinus betulus*) and members of the *Prunus* family.

HOW BAD IS IT? They are usually harmless, although perhaps rather unsightly.

PREVENTION AND CONTROL Prune the brooms out if they are causing offence.

See also

Fireblight (page 94).

Shot-hole borer

Sudden oak death

Witch's broom

Seed and cutting problems

Blackleg

This is a disease of cuttings, causing them to fail suddenly. The cutting base turns brown or black, shrinks and rots. The discoloration spreads upwards, affecting the whole cutting. Similar fungal infections cause damping off (*see* below).

PLANTS AFFECTED Cuttings of any plant are vulnerable, especially pelargoniums.

HOW BAD IS IT? Affected cuttings fail.

PREVENTION AND CONTROL Use clean pots, good potting compost and tap water for cuttings. Rainwater contains organisms that can prove harmful, as does unsterilized soil. Make sure your garden knife is clean. Rooting compounds speed up root formation, which may reduce the occurrence of blackleg.

Damping off

Damping off is a disease caused by a number of fungi and the main reason for failure in seedlings. They germinate well and start to grow thickly, then all of a sudden collapse and die. In a seed tray a patch of seedlings may die while the rest seem to be unaffected. If the disease hits before germination is complete, only a few seedlings may appear.

PLANTS AFFECTED All seedlings.

HOW BAD IS IT? If only patches of seedlings are affected, the rest may survive and grow big enough to be beyond damage. However, most are usually killed.

PREVENTION AND CONTROL Sow seed thinly in clean pots and good-quality compost. Water with fresh tap water, and do not overwater. Provide good ventilation and plenty of light. As a preventative measure, water seedlings with copper-based fungicides. Fungicide will not save infected seedlings.

Millipedes

Millipedes usually feed on rotting plant debris, but occasionally attack seedlings and other plants, especially those already damaged. They can be found in slug holes inside potatoes, for example. They are often confused with centipedes, but millipedes have two pairs of legs on each of their many body segments; centipedes have only one.

PLANTS AFFECTED Seedlings, some fruit, such as strawberries, and root vegetables such as potatoes.

HOW BAD IS IT? Seedlings usually die. Damage is unlikely to have been initiated by the millipede.

PREVENTION AND CONTROL Millipedes rarely cause great damage. Check under seed trays and oust any hiding there. Keep plant nurseries and cold frames clear of debris.

Woodlice

Like millipedes, woodlice are among nature's cleaners, living on rotting plant material, particularly wood. They like to cluster under pots in greenhouses though, where they may snack on seedlings and young plants. They also climb through drainage holes in pots, but should not cause any harm there. They can nibble bark around the base of trees wrapped with tree guards.

PLANTS AFFECTED Very young seedlings of any plants; plants soon grow too big to be damaged. Trees with tree guards.

HOW BAD IS IT? Damage is rare and not usually widespread.

PREVENTION AND CONTROL Tolerate woodlice as far as possible. Use pot feet to limit their numbers in the bases of pots, and flick out any hiding under seed trays. Check under tree guards; make sure these allow air circulation, since any woodlice are probably feeding on dying bark.

Blackleg

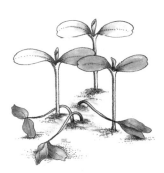

Damping off

Woodlice

Root and plant base problems

Cutworm

Narcissus bulb fly

Primula brown core

Cutworms

Cutworms are the larvae of several different moths, including species of *Agrotis* and *Noctua*. Their name is descriptive, since they cut through plants at their base, severing them from their roots and causing sudden wilting and death. The plants look undisturbed but have nothing connecting them to the soil (*see also* Vine weevil, opposite). Larger plants may have nibbled stem bases. Cutworms are pale brown or green and maggot-like; they hatch from early summer onwards.

PLANTS AFFECTED Many seedlings and young plants.

HOW BAD IS IT? Seedlings will be killed and young plants severely damaged, often beyond recovery.

PREVENTION AND CONTROL As soon as you notice damage, carefully dig around other plants in the vicinity, since these worms wriggle along to the next victim. Keep weeds to a minimum. Fork over soil to expose to birds.

Narcissus bulb fly

The maggot of the narcissus bulb fly develops inside bulbs of daffodils and other plants. The first sign of damage will be sparse leaf production and no flowers, and if the bulb is dug up and cut open it reveals a single maggot surrounded by brown excrement. This is the young of a hoverfly, from an egg laid in early summer of the previous year. (*See also* Eelworms, page 67.)

PLANTS AFFECTED Amaryllis (*Hippeastrum*), hyacinths, irises, daffodils (*Narcissus*) and snowdrops (*Galanthus*), as well as some vegetables, such as carrots, onions and potatoes.

HOW BAD IS IT? Any affected plants will not recover.

PREVENTION AND CONTROL Dig up and dispose of affected bulbs and other plants. Use horticultural fleece to protect bulbs after flowering, during late spring and early summer, when the fly is laying eggs. Cover the holes left by the dying leaves with soil to prevent the fly from gaining access to the centre of the bulb. Plant bulbs in shady spots, since the flies prefer sunshine.

Primula brown core

Brown core is a *Phytophthora* fungal disease of primulas and polyanthus. It attacks the base of plants, which grow too slowly and develop yellowing in the leaves. They wilt even when well watered. Investigation reveals that the roots have rotted away, particularly the finer roots. If you cut the remainder longitudinally, they have brown discoloration in their centres.

PLANTS AFFECTED Members of the *Primula* family, but particularly polyanthus.

HOW BAD IS IT? Plants do not recover and, since the fungus remains active in the surrounding soil, reinfection is likely.

PREVENTION AND CONTROL Dig up and destroy infected plants. Do not plant susceptible plants in the same area. There are no chemical treatments.

Rots

Plants suffer from various rotting diseases, usually caused by fungi taking hold when growing conditions are less than perfect or where specimens are already weak or diseased. Foot rots and root rots affect plants at the base, where they come into contact with the soil, and crown rots tend to kill the dormant buds of herbaceous plants, although they may also affect woody plants. Corms, bulbs and tubers, both ornamental and vegetable, may develop fungal problems in damp, poorly drained soil or during storage. The fungi involved are often *Fusarium*, *Verticillium* or *Phytophthora*. (*See also* Blackleg and Damping off, page 81, Fungal wilts, page 67 and Sclerotinia rot, page 79.)

PLANTS AFFECTED Many herbaceous and bulbous plants as well as young woody plants. Almost any plant growing in poor or over-wet conditions is susceptible.

HOW BAD IS IT? Once they have infected a plant, rots are often fatal, though early detection can save some.

PREVENTION AND CONTROL Most plants should be dug up and disposed of, particularly bulbs and corms, which will not recover. With clump-forming plants, it may be possible to salvage some uninfected parts by removing all diseased areas. Improve soil drainage. Before storing lifted bulbs for the winter, dust them with sulphur to prevent infection. Provide plants with good growing conditions, and plant corms, such as gladioli, in different situations each year to prevent the build-up of damaging soil organisms.

Swift moth caterpillar

There are several species of swift moth, but the caterpillars of garden swift moths and ghost swift moths are particular pests. Hatching from late spring until late summer, these white caterpillars live in the soil and feed on bulbs, corms, rhizomes and tubers, as well as the roots of other plants.

PLANTS AFFECTED Many herbaceous plants, particularly those with fleshy roots such as bulbs, corms, rhizomes or tubers.

HOW BAD IS IT? At best, plants lack vigour and wilt; at worst, they are killed.

PREVENTION AND CONTROL Dig carefully around sickly plants to check for and remove caterpillars. Whenever you find caterpillars while digging the soil (or any other grubs or maggots for that matter), pick them out and throw them to the birds. Chemical controls have very little effect.

Vine weevil

The small, white, curved larvae of the vine weevil, *Otiorhynchus sulcatus*, live just under the soil surface and make a meal of the roots of plants from late autumn until early spring. They are often found in the compost of pots in which overwintering plants have died mysteriously. Tubers are also targeted, as are indoor and greenhouse plants. The adult weevils are matt black with ribbed, dotted bodies. They feed on leaves at night, cutting large notches into the margins.

PLANTS AFFECTED Larvae eat any young plants, and tubers of cyclamen and begonias. Adults graze on bergenias, *Epimedium*, euonymus (evergreen varieties), hydrangeas, rhododendrons and strawberries.

HOW BAD IS IT? Larval damage is often fatal or at least severely debilitating; adult weevil damage is disfiguring.

PREVENTION AND CONTROL Encourage predators such as birds, frogs and hedgehogs. Keep adult numbers down through nightly inspections of plant pots. Place cloths under shrubs and give them a shake to dislodge any lurking in the branches. In greenhouses, use the biological controls *Steinernema kraussei* or *Heterorhabditis megidis* (*see* page 27). Inspect tubers before planting in spring, as larvae may be hiding in them. Crush adults and throw any larvae to the birds.

See also

Bacterial soft rot (page 109), Clematis wilt (page 76), Club root (page 110), Crown gall (page 77), Wireworm (page 113).

Foot rot

Swift moth caterpillar

Vine weevil

Bulb blindness

Camellia petal blight

Chrysanthemum blight

Flower problems

Bud drop

It is upsetting when flower buds drop off just when they look as if they are ready to bloom. The plant may look very healthy in other respects. (*See also* Rhododendron bud blast, opposite.)

PLANTS AFFECTED Camellias and rhododendrons; some container-grown woody plants, such as roses and fruit trees.

HOW BAD IS IT? Usually not all buds are affected, so you still get some flowers. Many camellias drop a few buds no matter how well they are grown.

PREVENTION AND CONTROL The most common cause is a dry spell – even just a few days – when the flower buds are forming, which is the end of the previous summer in the case of early-flowering plants. Water plants well and regularly, particularly those in containers, and mulch thickly to retain moisture.

Bulb blindness

Daffodils may grow plenty of healthy leaves but produce no flower buds. Alternatively, the flower stem emerges and is topped with the outer papery bud casing but this has no petals inside.

PLANTS AFFECTED Usually daffodils.

HOW BAD IS IT? This is usually just a cultivation problem, which can be rectified fairly simply. It could also be narcissus bulb fly or the bulb may have rotted (*see* page 82).

PREVENTION AND CONTROL Lift and divide affected clumps, refreshing the soil with compost. Water and feed bulbs before the leaves die down. Plant bulbs at the correct depth – two or three times deeper than the bulb's height. Leave fading leaves in place for at least six weeks after flowering has finished.

Camellia petal blight

This fungal disease affects flowers shortly after they open. The petals develop pale or darker spots that spread over the whole surface. Flowers drop early and carry black fungal growths, particularly at their base.

PLANTS AFFECTED Camellia.

HOW BAD IS IT? This is a persistent, unsightly disease. It can remain in the soil for five years and is hard to eradicate.

PREVENTION AND CONTROL A new disease in Britain, this currently occurs only in southern England. It is notifiable, so contact your local authority if you suspect your camellias have it. Burn fallen flowers and mulch around plants.

Chrysanthemum blight

There are two types of chrysanthemum blight, both appearing in autumn. The most common, chrysanthemum ray blight, is caused by the fungus *Didymella chrysanthemi* and attacks the ray petals, producing reddish spots. These grow and spread, soon infecting the entire flower-head, which then rots away. Shoot-tips can also droop and rot. Chrysanthemum petal blight, caused by *Itersonilia perplexans*, is rarer and produces smaller, browner spots.

PLANTS AFFECTED Chrysanthemums, particularly those in greenhouses; occasionally other members of the daisy family (Asteraceae).

HOW BAD IS IT? Both diseases disfigure, stunt and often kill affected plants.

PREVENTION AND CONTROL Dispose of plants. Sometimes damage can be limited if it is caught early on by pruning out infected areas. Increase air circulation and reduce humidity. Keep plant debris to a minimum to prevent the fungal spores from overwintering.

Frost and wind damage

Flowers that open early in the year are vulnerable to damage by cold, wet and windy weather, in combination or individually. An overnight frost can turn blooms and buds brown, and early leaves and shoots can also be damaged.

PLANTS AFFECTED Camellias, pieris, rhododendrons and early-flowering fruit trees such as plums and peaches. Other plants that make unusually early growth may also be affected.

HOW BAD IS IT? Brown and damaged flowers are unsightly; crops on fruit trees may be reduced or lost. Regular frosting of leaf shoots can permanently stunt plants or spoil their shape.

PREVENTION AND CONTROL Plant early-flowering shrubs in a sheltered spot. Site camellias especially out of early-morning sun. On frosty nights throw fleece or a light sheet over smaller plants, but remove it first thing in the morning. Where early leaf shoots are affected, an autumn application of sulphate of potash may help.

Peony wilt

This disease, caused by a botrytis species (*see* Grey mould, page 68), makes flower stems droop, shrink and turn brown just below the buds. The rest of the stem can appear normal. Affected buds do not open. The fungus causes similar wilting of leafy shoots. Sometimes webby, grey fungal growth is visible.

PLANTS AFFECTED Mainly herbaceous peonies, but sometimes tree peonies too.

HOW BAD IS IT? Where flower stems are affected it is disfiguring. Bad attacks can be debilitating and the disease may return.

PREVENTION AND CONTROL Remove affected stems to below soil level. Improve air circulation by thinning healthy growth if necessary – keep tools clean to avoid spreading infection. Clear old growth in autumn to prevent spores overwintering. Where the disease persists, try mulching or replace the soil around the plant's crown.

Pollen beetle

These black or brown beetles are most noticeable in spring and midsummer, when they can feed inside flowers. They usually eat small amounts of pollen from open blooms, but sometimes tunnel into buds.

PLANTS AFFECTED Yellow flowers, such as daffodils; members of the daisy family (Asteraceae), such as shasta daisies and dahlias, as well as roses and sweet peas (*Lathyrus*), runner beans and courgettes.

HOW BAD IS IT? They can be a nuisance on flowers cut to bring indoors.

PREVENTION AND CONTROL Give cut flowers a shake before bringing them in, or put them in a cool, dark shed the beetles should leave of their own accord.

Rhododendron bud blast

Brown, dry-looking buds covered with tiny, bristly pimples are symptomatic of bud blast, a fungus spread by leafhoppers (*see* page 69). The buds do not open and may remain on the shrub for several years.

PLANTS AFFECTED Rhododendrons.

HOW BAD IS IT? Usually not all buds are affected, so you will still have some flowers. The rest of the plant will remain healthy.

PREVENTION AND CONTROL Pick off as many dead buds as possible to prevent reinfection in summer, when leafhoppers start feeding. Reduce leafhopper numbers.

See also

Bird damage (page 99), Blind shoots (page 86), Blossom wilt (page 99), Capsid bug (page 65), Clematis wilt (page 76), Dieback (page 78), Fasciation (page 78).

Frost or wind damage

Peony wilt

Pollen beetle

Balling

Black spot

Leaf-cutter bee

Rose problems

Balling

Flower buds seem to be growing normally but then turn brown and papery and may stop plumping up. Affected buds fail to open and may develop fuzzy, mouldy growths. If you peel off the scorched outer petals, those inside are normal.

PLANTS AFFECTED Roses, particularly those with many thin petals.

HOW BAD IS IT? Usually only a few buds are affected, so the display will not be spoiled. Plants remain healthy otherwise.

PREVENTION AND CONTROL Balling occurs when warm, wet weather is followed by sunshine, so prevention is difficult. If you are watering your plants, do your watering in the evening and at the roots, not over the plant, to avoid exacerbating the problem. Remove affected buds to prevent dieback.

Black spot

One of the most common diseases of roses, black spot is also one of the most difficult to control. The leaves develop fuzzy-edged, black spots and quickly turn yellow. They often drop early. Damp, warm weather helps to spread the fungal spores, and the disease is often at its worst in midsummer.

PLANTS AFFECTED Roses, including wild varieties; some cultivars, notably from *Rosa rugosa*, are more resistant.

HOW BAD IS IT? The plant can be severely defoliated, and it will be weakened by successive attacks.

PREVENTION AND CONTROL Pick off affected leaves and burn fallen leaves. Give plants a high-potash feed, since potash deficiency may make black spot worse. Mulch to prevent the spores splashing up from the ground. Grow resistant varieties. Use sulphur fungicide at the first signs of infection. If black spot is a recurring

problem on plants, as a last resort use an approved synthetic fungicide; all will require repeated applications.

Blind shoots

Occasionally shoots fail to produce flower buds at their tips. Such shoots may have unusually small leaves and end abruptly or with small, rough, husk-like tissues. Surrounding stems develop normally and the plant looks otherwise healthy.

PLANTS AFFECTED Many roses; blindness also occurs in other flowering plants.

HOW BAD IS IT? Not a big problem.

PREVENTION AND CONTROL Prune out the affected shoot to about half its length, just above a healthy bud. It should reshoot and flower a bit later. Poor growing conditions may be the cause, so check your roses are getting all they need. Don't plant roses in frost pockets (*see* page 16).

Leaf-cutter bee

Neat semi-circles or half-ovals removed from the leaf edges are the work of the leaf-cutter bee. The shapes are distinctive and easy to tell from the less neat and accurate shapes made by caterpillars and other leaf-eating pests. Leaf-cutter bees use the leaf tissue to build cells for their larvae.

PLANTS AFFECTED Mainly roses, but also wisteria and other plants.

HOW BAD IS IT? Heavy attacks can be unsightly, but plants are rarely harmed.

PREVENTION AND CONTROL Keep your roses growing healthily and they should be able to cope with a certain amount of leaf-cutting. If a bee keeps returning to the same rose, consider covering the plant with horticultural fleece or fine netting for a week or so to discourage its activities.

Proliferation

Proliferation is an odd phenomenon in which normal-looking buds open to flowers that contain further buds, and sometimes even stems and leaves, developing at the centre the petals.

PLANTS AFFECTED Most commonly found on roses – some cultivars are particularly prone – but also other plants, such as pears and apples.

HOW BAD IS IT? The plant itself is not harmed in any way. You may choose to remove the affected flower or flowers, or leave them as a curiosity.

PREVENTION AND CONTROL There are different opinions about what causes proliferation. Some people believe it is environmental factors, such as a hard frost as the flower buds are forming, others that it is virus infection. It might even be a genetic error. Gardeners have little control over any of these, so prevention is difficult. Where many of the flowers on a sickly plant are repeatedly affected, it could be viral, in which case disposal is the best bet.

Rose canker and dieback

Grey mould (*see* page 68) and similar fungal diseases may attack roses in spring, when they are growing strongly. Affected stems look sickly and often develop a dark purple patch low down on the stem. This may spread over the whole shoot, which then dies back. Soft, grey fungal growth is sometimes seen in damp weather.

PLANTS AFFECTED Roses and many other plants. (*See also* Cankers, page 76, and Dieback, page 78.)

HOW BAD IS IT? Depending on how early it is treated, the plant may simply lose vigour or it could die.

PREVENTION AND CONTROL Remove affected shoots, cutting back into healthy tissue; this can mean to ground level. Use sharp secateurs, since poor pruning cuts can allow the disease access, and clean your tools between cuts. Ensure the rose has good growing conditions: lack of air circulation, poor drainage and excessive mulching too close to the stems all assist the spread of fungal infections.

Rose galls

Rose galls most often contain the grubs of *Diplolepis* gall wasps. The tangled type known as Robin's pincushions appear on the stems or leaves and are reminiscent of small, mossy pompons made from thick, red or yellow-green threads. Others, like spiny galls, pea galls and spiky 'sputnik' galls, can also appear on leaves.

PLANTS AFFECTED Most common on wild or species roses.

HOW BAD IS IT? Harmless, but possibly considered unsightly. Only the crown gall (*see* page 77) is a serious problem.

PREVENTION AND CONTROL Remove the galls if they offend you.

Rose leafhopper

Like other leafhoppers (*see* page 69), rose leafhoppers and their young feed on leaf sap. They are pale yellow with the typical long, tapering body. Large infestations turn the leaves yellow and are particularly harmful in a hot summer, especially in roses growing in sheltered conditions.

PLANTS AFFECTED Roses.

HOW BAD IS IT? Leaves become pale and the plant's vigour is reduced.

PREVENTION AND CONTROL Pick off the larvae. Spray with pyrethrum, fatty acids or plant oils in early or mid-spring, before infestations take off. Make several applications. As a last resort, use an approved chemical pesticide.

Proliferation

Robin's pincushion gall

Spiny gall (left) **and pea gall** (right)

Rose-leaf-rolling sawfly

This sawfly attacks in early summer, especially in hot weather. The female injects the leaves with a toxin as she lays her egg, causing the edges to roll down tightly around it. The emerging grub eats the leaf, or the leaf may simply shrivel and dry out.

PLANTS AFFECTED Roses.

HOW BAD IS IT? A heavy infestation can be debilitating.

PREVENTION AND CONTROL If only a few leaves are affected, pick them off. In heavier infestations, it may better to use an approved systemic pesticide. Keep soil beneath plants clear of weeds in winter to expose larvae to birds.

Rose-leaf-rolling sawfly

Rose powdery mildew

Rose powdery mildew is one of several fungi that cause powdery mildew (*see* page 70). Most thrive where the soil is dry but the surrounding air is moist. A white powder develops on young leaves, under which the leaf surface soon becomes pale and yellowing; the leaves are usually distorted and stunted. Roses seem to be particularly susceptible to powdery mildew – or maybe the mildew species that infects them is particularly persistent, and helped by the way we often grow roses against walls and fences, where they are likely to be dry at the roots due to rain shadow (*see* page 17). Brick walls are usually worst.

PLANTS AFFECTED Roses.

HOW BAD IS IT? Apart from being very disfiguring, rose powdery mildew can stop the flower buds from opening. The leaves often fall early, which has a debilitating effect.

PREVENTION AND CONTROL Choose resistant varieties for sites likely to encourage mildew. Plant roses well,

Rose powdery mildew

adding plenty of organic matter, and mulch them at least annually. In dry weather, water regularly into the soil around the base of the plant, avoiding the foliage. Prune plants to keep an open structure that allows air circulation. If powdery mildew appears, prune out infected shoots and use soft soap or sulphur powder or sprays to limit its spread. Clear up fallen leaves. As a last resort, spray with fungicides to clear infections or as a preventative.

Rose replant sickness

As a rule, if a plant dies of a disease, it's not a good idea to plant the same sort of plant in the same place because the disease could still be lurking in the soil. This rule applies strongly to roses, which suffer from a problem called replant sickness. This happens when new roses fail to thrive where roses have already been grown, even if it was some years before, and even if the old roses seemed healthy. The cause may be eelworms (*see* page 67) transmitting viruses, or some kind of fungal infection.

PLANTS AFFECTED Roses.

HOW BAD IS IT? At the very least the new plant will fail to thrive, at worst it will die. Roses that show signs of replant sickness may be saved by digging them up, removing as much soil as possible and replanting elsewhere.

PREVENTION AND CONTROL Choose a different planting site. If this is not possible, remove the existing soil, taking out a hole at least 45cm (18in) square and deep, and replace it with new. Replant sickness may be exacerbated by lack of nutrients, so add mycorrhizal fungal granules (*see* page 21) and plenty of nitrogen fertilizer to the planting hole and feed your new roses regularly.

Rose replant sickness

Rose rust

This fungal disease appears from midsummer. It produces clusters of bright orange spores on the leaf undersides, with matching yellow-orange spots on the upper leaf surfaces. The stems may also be infected with crusty, spore-laden scabs that cause cracking in the bark, which will let in secondary infections. Overwintering spores are brown-black. The disease may appear as early as spring but worsens throughout the year.

PLANTS AFFECTED Roses.

HOW BAD IS IT? This is an ugly disease causing early leaf drop and reduced vigour, though flowers are still produced. It can be persistent.

PREVENTION AND CONTROL Prune out early signs of rust, particularly where it appears on the stems. Remove fallen leaves in autumn and then mulch around the plant to prevent reinfection. The spores may also overwinter on supports, so consider changing these. As a last resort, spray both surfaces of leaves with a fungicide as a preventative measure or to treat infections. You will need to make repeated applications until late summer.

Rose slugworm

The larvae of some sawflies (*see* page 72) are known as slugworms because of their slug-like appearance. Slugworms can appear on rose leaves, and some look less slug-like and more like small, tapering, green caterpillars that are fatter at the head end. All slugworms feed by scraping off the outer tissues of leaves, leaving a 'skeleton' behind that soon dries off and turns brown. They usually feed on the leaf underside, but sometimes the upper sides are eaten too.

PLANTS AFFECTED Roses. Other species attack fruit trees (*see* page 97).

HOW BAD IS IT? A heavy infestation soon damages leaves, which do not recover and look unattractive, but this pest is relatively easy to control.

PREVENTION AND CONTROL Pick off any larvae that you see. If necessary, spray the leaves with pyrethrum-based insecticides. As a last resort, use a systemic insecticide.

Rose virus

There are several viruses that infect roses, but fortunately they rarely seem to be as serious as some other viruses appearing on ornamental plants (*see* page 74) or crops (*see* page 97). The symptoms vary, but most create yellowing between the veins or spread out across the whole leaf in swirling lines. The yellowing may be distinct or virtually invisible.

PLANTS AFFECTED Roses.

HOW BAD IS IT? Plants may be stunted or distorted, but if they are not, you might choose to live with it.

PREVENTION AND CONTROL There are no controls. Make sure your plants have good growing conditions and keep up with pruning and feeding, and they should be able to shrug off attacks. Inadvertent weedkiller damage can produce similar effects, so make sure this has not occurred. Viruses are spread by sap-sucking insects, mainly aphids, which is one major reason to control these pests (*see* page 64).

See also

Aphids (page 64), Bud drop (page 84), Caterpillars (page 66), Coral spot (page 77), Crown gall (page 77), Eelworms (page 67), Fasciation (page 78), Honeydew (page 68), Honey fungus (page 79), Leaf miners (page 69), Pollen beetle (page 85), Red spider mite (page 71), Thrips (page 73).

Rose rust

Rose slugworm

Rose virus

Vegetables and fruit

American gooseberry mildew

Pests and diseases of fruit and vegetables can be infuriating, especially when you're hoping for abundant crops. Leaves often show the first symptoms, but any plant parts may be affected. This section covers leaf problems (pages 90–7), stem and bark problems (page 98), flower problems (page 99), fruit problems (pages 100–5), tomato problems (pages 106–8) and root and plant base problems (pages 109–13).

Leaf problems

American gooseberry mildew

Like other powdery mildews (*see* page 70), this fungal infection produces a white, powdery coating on the upper surface of the leaves. It also covers the stems and causes distortion of the shoot-tips and dieback. Where the fruit are infected, the powder is pale brown.
PLANTS AFFECTED Gooseberries and blackcurrants.
HOW BAD IS IT? Cleaned fruits are still edible, but turn brown when cooked. Prolonged attacks weaken plants.
PREVENTION AND CONTROL Cut out infected branches. Prune plants annually to ensure good air circulation. Do not overuse nitrogen-rich fertilizers, which can encourage the disease; give a dose of sulphate of potash in spring instead of general-purpose fertilizer. Some gooseberry varieties such as 'Greenfinch', 'Hinomaki Red' and 'Pax' are resistant.

Aphid

Aphids

In the veg garden aphids attack a number of plants, causing damage similar to that in ornamentals (*see* page 64). Signs also include, for example, raised red-stained areas on currant leaves produced by currant blister aphids, and curled young leaves on apple trees caused by pink-coloured rosy apple aphids. The insects are most commonly found feeding on leaf undersides and young shoots. Broad beans are nearly always infested by blackfly, which cluster at the top of the plants.
PLANTS AFFECTED Many, including broad beans, currants (particularly redcurrants), gooseberries, lettuces, raspberries, shallots.
HOW BAD IS IT? Heavy infestations affect the vigour and appearance of plants, and may decrease yields. On leafy vegetables they can reduce edibility.
PREVENTION AND CONTROL Encourage natural predators, such as ladybird larvae, hoverfly larvae and parasitic wasps, into your garden. Keep numbers down by rubbing infested leaves and buds with your fingers. Pinch out the soft tips of broad beans to remove the problem. If necessary, spray with pyrethrum, soft or insecticidal soap or plant oils. As a last resort, use a chemical pesticide approved for crops.

Asparagus beetle

The beetle is red and black with white or yellow blotches on its back. Both it and its larvae feed on the skin of asparagus leaves and stems. Growth above damage will die.

Asparagus beetle

PLANTS AFFECTED Asparagus.

HOW BAD IS IT? Concerted attacks affect vigour and reduce yields.

PREVENTION AND CONTROL Pick off beetles and larvae when you see them if possible. Cut off and burn stems at the end of the season to prevent this pest from overwintering. If necessary, spray with pyrethrum during the growing season.

Bean halo blight

This bacterial disease is usually brought into the garden on seeds, and produces browning in the seed leaves. If plants survive to produce 'true' leaves, these will have yellow spots that look slightly oily or water-soaked in their centre.

PLANTS AFFECTED Dwarf French beans and runner beans.

HOW BAD IS IT? Yield will be affected, especially if the pods are infected.

PREVENTION AND CONTROL Do not soak seeds before sowing, since this may encourage the bacteria. Remove infected leaves as soon as you spot a problem. Avoid wetting the leaves by watering at the roots, not from overhead. Burn infected plants at the end of the year, rather than composting them. In future, grow beans with some resistance, such as dwarf 'Eden' and 'Fandango' or runner 'Red Rum'.

Bird damage

Birds often have an eye on your vegetable patch as a place for an easy meal. Pigeons are very fond of brassicas and can make short work of young plants during the winter, when food is scarce elsewhere. They usually strip all the soft leaf tissue from around the tougher midrib.

PLANTS AFFECTED Brussels sprouts, cabbages and cauliflowers. Fruit is also taken, and even flowers (see page 99).

HOW BAD IS IT? Pigeons are large birds and badly damaged plants will not recover. Damage is likely to be greater during cold weather, when they are more hungry.

PREVENTION AND CONTROL Protect the crop with netting, particularly when it is young. Netting can be draped over plants, but it is better fixed over a rigid frame.

Blackcurrant big bud mite

Microscopic, white mites infest the buds of blackcurrants during the winter. Their feeding activities make the buds swell and grow much larger than usual; they are also rounded, whereas normal buds are pointed.

PLANTS AFFECTED Blackcurrants; hazel (Corylus) and yew (Taxus) have similar pests.

HOW BAD IS IT? The buds do not develop normally, so are useless to the plant, which will lose vigour. Most important, the mites may spread reversion virus (see page 94).

PREVENTION AND CONTROL Pick off swollen buds as soon as you see them. Dig up and destroy badly infected plants. Grow blackcurrant 'Ben Hope', which is resistant.

Blackcurrant gall midge

The small, maggoty larvae of the blackcurrant gall midge damage the young growth of blackcurrants in three phases from spring through summer. Their feeding activities distort and kill the foliage and shoot-tips, and this may encourage many smaller sideshoots to grow.

PLANTS AFFECTED Blackcurrants.

HOW BAD IS IT? The worst damage occurs in late spring, when growth should be at its strongest and the plants are flowering. Crops may be badly depleted.

PREVENTION AND CONTROL There are no chemical controls. If your plants regularly suffer attacks, grow the resistant varieties 'Ben Connan' and 'Ben Sarek'.

Bean halo blight

Blackcurrant big bud mite

Blackcurrant gall midge

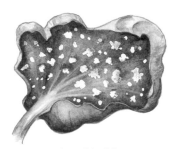

Brassica whiptail

Brassica whiptail

Brassica leaves are usually large and thick, with an overall rounded shape. Whiptail is a physiological condition that makes them grow long and narrow, almost ribbon-like, with long stems.

PLANTS AFFECTED Members of the brassica family, but particularly cauliflower and sprouting broccoli.

HOW BAD IS IT? Crops are usually spoiled. Heads of cauliflower or broccoli may be very small or not form at all.

PREVENTION AND CONTROL The problem is caused by a lack of the trace element molybdenum (*see* page 25). It usually occurs on acid soils. Brassicas prefer alkaline soils, so add lime before growing them and a slow-release fertilizer that contains trace elements.

Brassica white blister

In this fungal disease of the brassica family, raised, blister-like spots appear on the leaf undersides, sometimes in concentric circles. They are usually white and shiny. The upper surface has corresponding yellow pitting. As with many fungal infections, *Albugo candida* thrives during mild, damp weather but it may also be spread by insects.

PLANTS AFFECTED Brassicas, such as cabbage, cauliflower and broccoli, and some related ornamentals, such as honesty (*Lunaria*).

HOW BAD IS IT? The leaves become misshapen as they grow, because of the distorting effects of the infected areas. Yields are not greatly reduced and unaffected parts will be edible.

PREVENTION AND CONTROL Pick off any leaves showing signs of infection. If plants are badly diseased, dig them up. Increase spacing between plants to improve air circulation and practise crop rotation. Grow resistant varieties such as Brussels sprout 'Exodus F1' and broccoli 'Green Magic'.

Brassica wire stem

Wire stem is caused by the fungus *Rhizoctonia solani*. Like damping off (*see* page 81), it invades the stems of young plants. It appears as a dark patch on the stem, which soon turns dark red-brown and becomes slender and wiry. The roots are surrounded by webby fungal growth.

PLANTS AFFECTED Any members of the brassica family, especially cauliflower and broccoli. Seedlings are particularly prone.

HOW BAD IS IT? Seedlings are usually killed. Older plants may survive, but their growth will be very slow and they may never make good crops.

PREVENTION AND CONTROL Poor growing conditions contribute to the onset of this disease, particularly dry soil. Plant seeds in good-quality potting compost and do not put seedlings into the garden soil until they are growing well and a good size. Do not overfeed. Dig up and dispose of infected plants.

Broad bean chocolate spot

Distinctive brown flecks and spots appear on the leaves of broad beans, particularly the upper surfaces. They may spread onto the stems and pods. The cause is a fungal disease in the botrytis family (*see* page 68).

PLANTS AFFECTED Broad beans.

HOW BAD IS IT? At best, yields will be affected. At worst, seedlings and even larger plants will die.

PREVENTION AND CONTROL Give seedlings lots of space. Choose an airy spot, as the fungus spreads faster in damp conditions. As a preventative, spray with a fungicide based on plant and fish oils.

Broad bean chocolate spot

Caterpillars

Many moths and butterflies target vegetable gardens for egg-laying, since the crops provide a ready food source for their young. Leaves, pods, fruit, bark and stems may all be eaten or tunnelled into (*see also* pages 98 and 102). Cabbage white butterflies – both large and small – are perhaps the best-known leaf-eaters, laying their neat clusters of eggs under brassica leaves. Cabbage moth caterpillars also attack brassicas and onions, while those of the leek moth are leaf miners (*see* page 69), feeding within onion and leek leaves.

PLANTS AFFECTED Many, including brassicas and the onion family.

HOW BAD IS IT? Depending on the plant, damage can be great. For example, caterpillars may eat the hearts out of cabbages, ruining the crop for eating.

PREVENTION AND CONTROL Pick off caterpillars wherever possible. Use horticultural fleece to protect vulnerable crops, such as leeks. A few caterpillars, such as cabbage whites and cabbage moth, may be sprayed with pyrethrum or a chemical pesticide approved for crops if necessary. Do this as soon as you spot them; when they get into the heart of plants, insecticides will not reach them.

Celery heart rot

The hearts of celery turn brown and rot away, leaving a slimy mess at the centre of the plant. This condition is more common in hot, dry summers, and may not be noticed until the celery is harvested.

PLANTS AFFECTED Celery.

HOW BAD IS IT? Crops will be inedible.

PREVENTION AND CONTROL Heart rot is usually caused by a lack of calcium, which can be caused by overfeeding with high-nitrogen fertilizer. Apply a foliar feed that contains a calcium supplement. Grow plants in very humus-rich ground and give them plenty of water. Even provide a little shade in a hot summer.

Celery leaf miner

The celery leaf miner is a fly larva that behaves in much the same way as other leaf miners (*see* page 69) in that it feeds between the leaf tissues, which then turn brown and die.

PLANTS AFFECTED Celery, celeriac, lovage, parsley and parsnip.

HOW BAD IS IT? Damage is usually only cosmetic, and crops are not affected, but heavy infestations can spoil more delicate crops that rely on growing fast to retain their tenderness.

PREVENTION AND CONTROL Pick off affected leaves to reduce fly populations. Place horticultural fleece or fine crop-protection netting over plants to prevent the fly laying its eggs in the first place.

Colorado beetle

Colorado beetle is not established in Britain and Ireland, but has been a threat for many years and is now common throughout the rest of Europe. This small, yellow-and-black-striped beetle and its red larvae eat the foliage of a range of vegetables.

PLANTS AFFECTED Aubergines, peppers, potatoes, tomatoes; other plants in the potato (Solanaceae) family.

HOW BAD IS IT? This is a potentially devastating pest, particularly of potatoes.

PREVENTION AND CONTROL Fortunately, Colorado beetle is unlikely to appear on your crops, but it does sometimes arrive in Britain via imported vegetables, such as salads and herbs. It is a notifiable pest, so if you find it contact your local council immediately; they will advise you on what to do.

Caterpillar

Celery leaf miner

Colorado beetle

Currant reversion virus

Currant reversion virus

This is a viral disease that may be brought into your garden by blackcurrant big bud mite (*see* page 91). The leaves of affected plants are smaller than usual and often somewhat yellow. They may also have fewer lobes than normal. Check for enlarged buds, which indicate the presence of the mite.

PLANTS AFFECTED Blackcurrants.

HOW BAD IS IT? Cropping will be poor. Plants do not recover and should be removed and destroyed.

PREVENTION AND CONTROL There are no controls. Always buy currant plants from reputable sources. 'Ben Hope' is resistant to big bud mite, so should be less likely to contract reversion virus.

Fireblight

This is a serious bacterial disease that usually first appears when the flowers open, since it gains entry into the plants through them. Flowers and leaves die, but the disease quickly spreads. On young stems it produces sunken areas that may ooze a slimy, white liquid. Under the bark, these areas are usually stained foxy red. The plant develops a scorched appearance.

PLANTS AFFECTED Fruit-bearing members of the Rosaceae family, including apples and pears; this also includes cotoneaster, hawthorn and pyracantha.

HOW BAD IS IT? Plants can be severely affected and may die if the disease is not caught early.

PREVENTION AND CONTROL Prune out infected stems. On small branches, remove the infected wood and about 30cm (12in) of healthy growth below it; on larger branches, increase this to 60cm (24in). Peel bark to ensure you are into healthy wood. Dig up and destroy small or badly infected plants.

Fireblight

Gooseberry sawfly

Gooseberry sawfly

The larvae of three species of sawfly make an easy meal of gooseberry leaves from mid- or late spring onwards. Looking like small, pale green caterpillars, sometimes with black spotting, the larvae feed voraciously from the centre of the bushes, where the eggs are laid, outwards. Damage starts in late spring, but there can be two or three generations of larvae, causing damage later in the season.

PLANTS AFFECTED Gooseberries, redcurrants and whitecurrants.

HOW BAD IS IT? The damage can be extensive. Some bushes will be defoliated in a very short space of time.

PREVENTION AND CONTROL Check the inner leaves for eggs and larvae from mid-spring. Remove and destroy larvae where possible. Use pyrethrum sprays if necessary. As a last resort, use a synthetic pesticide approved for fruit crops.

Leek white tip

A fungus in the *Phytophthora* family, *P. porri*, is responsible for this disease, which causes dieback in the leaves towards the end of summer and into autumn. Dieback starts as yellowing in the leaf ends and progresses down the leaves; these may turn pale brown or white and eventually dry out, or they may rot. The bulb or plant base may also start to rot.

PLANTS AFFECTED Any in the onion family, particularly leeks, onions and ornamental alliums.

HOW BAD IS IT? Infected plants are soon rendered inedible and die. Dig them up as soon as you see the infection.

PREVENTION AND CONTROL Remove plants to prevent spread of the disease. Do not grow leeks or related plants in the same spot, or near by, for at least five years. There are no chemical controls.

Onion eelworm

Onion eelworms infest all parts of onion plants, including the bulbs and seeds, causing stunted, contorted growth and odd swellings. Eelworms (*see also* page 67) are microscopic worms. They invade plant tissues, which become soft and may have a mealy texture. Developing bulbs may split and rots soon set in.

PLANTS AFFECTED Garlic, onions and spring onions. Beans, carrots, parsnips and peas can harbour eelworms without showing symptoms, as can weeds.

HOW BAD IS IT? Plants infested early in the season usually die. Those affected later may still produce bulbs but these will not store well.

PREVENTION AND CONTROL Remove and destroy infested plants. Buy onion sets from reputable sources. Use crop rotation and keep your vegetable garden free of weeds. Grow lettuces or brassicas in the infected site to clean it up.

Pea and bean weevil

These tiny, grey-brown, ridged and dotted beetles feed around the leaf edges, making distinctive U-shaped notches. The larvae live in the soil around the plants, feeding on the nitrogen-fixing nodules on the roots of leguminous plants.

PLANTS AFFECTED Only broad beans and peas.

HOW BAD IS IT? Unless infestations are very heavy, plants usually crop as normal.

PREVENTION AND CONTROL There is rarely any need to do anything about these weevils. Cover rows of young plants with fleece until they are large enough to shrug off attacks. As a last resort, where large infestations are affecting seedlings and young plants, use pyrethrum or a chemical pesticide approved for vegetable crops to reduce their numbers.

Peach leaf curl

Peach leaf curl is caused by a fungus with spores that overwinter in the bark and buds of plants. The disease infects the new leaves as they unfurl in spring, producing blistering with red or purple discoloration. White powder spreads over the leaves and they soon drop. Trees put out a second flush of leaves, which is usually unaffected.

PLANTS AFFECTED Almonds, apricots, nectarines and peaches; sometimes ornamental cherries (*Prunus*).

HOW BAD IS IT? It is very unsightly. One-off attacks can be shrugged off; repeated attacks over successive years will reduce vigour and cropping.

PREVENTION AND CONTROL Pick off infected leaves and give plants food and water to encourage plenty of healthy new growth. Cover trees growing against walls with plastic sheeting from midwinter to late spring to protect them from air-borne spores. (Use a frame to keep the sheeting off the new leaves.) As a preventative, use a copper-based fungicide in autumn before leaf fall and again in mid- and late winter.

Pear leaf blister mite

This microscopic gall mite eats the inner tissues of the leaves, mainly feeding immediately either side of the central leaf veins. The first signs are yellow or pink blisters in mid- to late spring, which turn black as the summer progresses. (*See also* Galls, page 62.)

PLANTS AFFECTED Pears.

HOW BAD IS IT? Although it is very unattractive, the damage does not affect the general health or cropping of the tree.

PREVENTION AND CONTROL On smaller trees, damaged leaves can be removed to improve the plant's appearance. Otherwise, you simply have to live with it, since there are no controls.

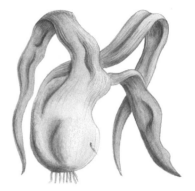

Onion eelworm

Pea and bean weevil

Pear leaf blister mite

Potato blight

Bean rust

Plum rust

Potato blight

One of the most devastating diseases in the vegetable garden, potato blight can kill plants overnight. It is caused by a *Phytophthora* fungus, *P. infestans*, which invades the foliage and rapidly causes brown patches of dying tissue. The foliage yellows and wilts and the stems turn brown or black and soon collapse.

PLANTS AFFECTED Potatoes and tomatoes (*see* page 106).

HOW BAD IS IT? Always fatal. It may be possible to save crops later in the season by removing all the top-growth as soon as the blight is spotted. Tubers that have already formed may escape infection, but check them regularly once in storage.

PREVENTION AND CONTROL Practise crop rotation and use deep earthing-up to protect tubers. Warm, damp weather encourages blight: during this sort of weather, use Bordeaux mixture or other copper-based fungicides as a preventative. Once blight has appeared, these are useless. Grow early potatoes, which are lifted before blight usually strikes, or resistant cultivars, such as those in the 'Sarpo' range.

Potato cyst eelworm

The first sign of infection by either white or golden potato cyst eelworm is when a few plants growing near each other start dying from the base upwards, the leaves soon yellowing. Tiny, white, yellow or brown lumps grow out from the roots. These are the female cyst eelworms, which are full of eggs.

PLANTS AFFECTED Potatoes and sometimes tomatoes.

HOW BAD IS IT? Affected plants will not crop and will soon die.

PREVENTION AND CONTROL Practise crop rotation to prevent a build-up of the problem in the first place. Rotation is ineffective once cyst eelworms have become established, because the cysts remain alive but dormant in the soil for many years. They are triggered into activity when potatoes are next grown in the vicinity. There are cultivars that are resistant to one type or the other, but rarely both.

Rusts

Like ornamental plants (*see* page 71), vegetables and fruits suffer from fungal diseases that produce rust-like pustules on the leaves and stems. The appearance of these can vary: on beans rust is dark brown, on leeks it is bright orange. Both cause dieback in the affected leaves, although plants may still grow and crop. Pustules on gooseberries are orange-red and usually affect older leaves, which curl and distort. Plum rust is brown under the leaf but can turn the upper surface yellow, and leaves will fall early.

PLANTS AFFECTED French and runner beans, leeks, and gooseberries and plums. The popular plum variety 'Victoria' is particularly susceptible.

HOW BAD IS IT? Rust is disfiguring and often debilitating. However, in most cases crops are not badly affected. Plum trees may be weakened if the attacks are severe and regular.

PREVENTION AND CONTROL Pay attention to the recommended spacings when planting, and increase air circulation around plants. Use crop rotation. On beans and gooseberries, remove affected parts. Avoid feeding leeks with high-nitrogen fertilizers, and use sulphate of potash when you plant them; this produces harder growth that can fend off rust. Leeks 'Apollo', 'Neptune' and 'Walton Mammoth' are resistant. Feed plum trees and rake up fallen leaves to limit reinfection.

Silver leaf disease

This fungal disease produces a silver tint in the upper surfaces of leaves. At first, just one or two branches may be affected, often near recent cuts or breaks. If stems are cut, you will see that the inner tissues are often stained brown.

PLANTS AFFECTED Members of the *Prunus* family, such as cherries and plums.

HOW BAD IS IT? If caught and treated very early, some trees may recover, otherwise the outlook is generally poor.

PREVENTION AND CONTROL Prune susceptible trees only when they are growing strongly so that cuts heal quickly. Keep pruning tools scrupulously clean. Remove infected areas, cutting at least 15cm (6in) into healthy wood (that is, beyond where staining ends).

Slugworms

Like small slugs, but thicker at the head end, these infest fruit trees from late spring, feeding on the leaves. They rasp away the upper leaf surface, leaving the remaining tissues to dry off and turn brown. They are the larvae of sawflies (*see* page 72).

PLANTS AFFECTED Cherries, pears, plums; also rowan (*Sorbus*).

HOW BAD IS IT? Small infestations rarely cause any problems and they do not eat the fruit.

PREVENTION AND CONTROL Where infestations are large on small trees, spray with pyrethrum. As a last resort, use a chemical pesticide approved for crops.

Strawberry eelworm

When eelworms infest strawberry plants, they cause reddening of the leaf stalks. These may be longer than normal, or shorter and thicker. The unusual reddening effect has led to the name red plant disease. A similar-looking condition, caused by fungal infection, is called red core.

PLANTS AFFECTED Strawberries.

HOW BAD IS IT? Infested plants will die.

PREVENTION AND CONTROL Dig up and destroy affected plants. Grow strawberries elsewhere for at least five years.

Viruses

Many virus diseases can infect vegetable plants, causing discoloration and distortion of leaves. In cucumber mosaic, for example, the leaves are covered with yellow mottling, while in carrot motley dwarf they are pink or yellow and often twisted.

PLANTS AFFECTED Many, including lettuces, onions, parsnips, peas, potatoes, raspberries and shallots.

HOW BAD IS IT? Plants are stunted, fail to thrive, flower or crop, and usually die, or should in any case be destroyed.

PREVENTION AND CONTROL Dig up and destroy infected plants. Weed regularly, since many weeds carry viruses without showing symptoms. Reduce insect pests where possible, particularly aphids (*see* page 64). Grow resistant varieties if available. Avoid spreading viruses yourself by keeping tools scrupulously clean and washing your hands after handling infected plants.

Silver leaf disease

Slugworm

See also

Algae (page 64), Downy mildew (page 66), False silver leaf (page 62), Flea beetles (page 67), Fungal wilts (page 67), Galls (page 62), Grey mould (page 68), Honeydew and sooty mould (page 68), Leafhoppers (page 69), Leaf miners (page 69), Leaf spots (page 69), Leaf weevils (page 69), Powdery mildew (page 70), Red spider mite (page 71), Shot-hole disease (page 72), Smuts (page 72), Snails and slugs (page 73), Tarsonemid mites (page 73), Spur blight (page 98), Sweetcorn smut (page 105), Thrips (page 73), Whitefly (page 74).

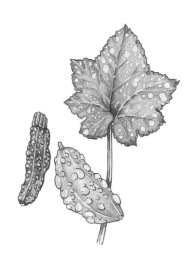

Cucumber mosaic virus

Cane spot

Raspberry cane blight

Spur blight

Stem and bark problems

Cane spot

This is a fungal disease that invades the canes of soft fruit, producing purple, canker-like pits with white centres on the bark in early summer. In severe cases the infection may spread to the leaves and flower stalks. (*See also* Cankers, page 76.)
PLANTS AFFECTED Loganberries and raspberries.
HOW BAD IS IT? Where cane spot takes hold, it can kill canes. The fruit of loganberries may be spoiled.
PREVENTION AND CONTROL Remove infected canes when you see them. Follow recommended pruning techniques, which offer the opportunity to remove offending canes too. As a last resort, spray with a copper-based fungicide. Some cultivars are particularly susceptible, including older types like 'Lloyd George', while the new 'Julia' has all-round disease-resistance.

Caterpillars

Although caterpillars usually eat leaves and fruit, some can cause trouble by feeding on stems and bark. The white caterpillars of the currant clearwing moth tunnel into stems to feed, which will weaken the stems. Raspberries are attacked by similar, but red, caterpillars. They live in the soil over winter, migrating into the stems in late spring.
PLANTS AFFECTED Redcurrants, blackcurrants, raspberries.
HOW BAD IS IT? Stems are usually weakened and may die back. Fortunately, infestations are usually limited to a few stems on any plant.
PREVENTION AND CONTROL Remove and burn or otherwise destroy weakened stems; they may snap of their own accord, indicating the presence of caterpillars.

Raspberry cane blight

This fungal disease can get into canes via frost damage, splits in the bark or feeding damage from cane midge, a tiny insect that feeds on raspberry canes. The blight often starts at the base of a cane, which becomes dark brown, and then causes the tips to die back. Tiny, black fruiting bodies appear on the dead areas.
PLANTS AFFECTED Raspberries.
HOW BAD IS IT? Damage can be widespread and serious, affecting crops and the plant's overall health.
PREVENTION AND CONTROL Prevent problems by careful pruning and training of plants. Keep pest numbers down and protect plants from frost. Prune out infected canes as soon as you see them, keeping your tools scrupulously clean.

Spur blight

This fungal disease appears as dark purple stains around the leaf buds of new canes and spreads along the canes, turning grey in autumn and producing tiny, black fruiting bodies.
PLANTS AFFECTED Raspberries.
HOW BAD IS IT? Very few leaves appear, shoots are weak and crops are very poor.
PREVENTION AND CONTROL Avoid overfeeding, since nitrogen is thought to encourage this disease, which flourishes in damp weather. Prune out infected canes and reduce cane numbers overall to improve air circulation.

See also

Cankers (page 76), Coral spot (page 77), Crown gall (page 77), Dieback (page 78), Fasciation (page 78), Fireblight (page 94), Honey fungus (page 79), Sclerotinia rot (page 79), Shot-hole borer (page 80), Squirrels (page 80).

Flower problems

Apple sucker

The apple sucker lays its eggs in leaf scars and bark crannies in autumn. The young hatch out in early spring just as apple trees come into leaf, and feed on the developing blooms. Reminiscent of lice, the nymphs are flat and pale green. The adults look like aphids and appear after the flowers have faded.

PLANTS AFFECTED Apples.

HOW BAD IS IT? The flowers turn brown, as if suffering from frost damage (*see* page 85), and fail to set fruit.

PREVENTION AND CONTROL On larger trees spraying is difficult, so this pest may have to be tolerated. If apple suckers are a frequent pest on smaller trees, consider spraying with pyrethrum when flowers are still green buds. As a last resort, use a suitable chemical pesticide.

Bird damage

Bullfinches eat the flower buds of many fruit trees in autumn and winter, while blackbirds, starlings and thrushes may all take a liking to ripening fruit and vegetables before you can harvest them.

PLANTS AFFECTED Flower buds of apples, cherries, gooseberries and pears; forsythia too. Apples, cherries, currants, peas, pears, plums and strawberries.

HOW BAD IS IT? Buds may be entirely stripped, although usually some remain at the shoot-tips to develop in spring. Crops, particularly of cherries, currants and strawberries, can be taken or be damaged beyond edibility.

PREVENTION AND CONTROL Use a fruit cage for all smaller fruit plants. Throw netting over parts of larger plants to protect a few fruit or secure net bags around a few of the better bunches.

Blossom wilt

This fungal disease affects flowers soon after they open. The blooms wither and die but may remain on the tree, allowing the infection to spread to leaves, which also die. Sometimes stems also die back. A close look at dead or dying parts reveals tiny, pale brown fungal fruiting bodies.

PLANTS AFFECTED Apples, apricots, cherries, peaches and plums; also the ornamental amelanchiers.

HOW BAD IS IT? Fruit crops are reduced. The fungus may overwinter and reinfect the tree, gradually weakening it.

PREVENTION AND CONTROL Prune out infected blooms immediately to avoid the disease spreading to leaves and stems. Keep an eye on these and remove any that show subsequent infection. Remove any cankers (*see* page 76). Keep tools clean.

Nectar-robbing bees

Some bee species cannot reach flowers' nectar in the normal way, so they chew a small hole in the flower base to get to it. Short-tongued bumblebee species may resort to this technique on some flowers. Other insects may then use the hole, leaving the flower unpollinated.

PLANTS AFFECTED Runner beans; some ornamentals, such as snapdragons (*Antirrhinum*), and strawberry tree (*Arbutus unedo*).

HOW BAD IS IT? Unpollinated flowers do not set fruit, but usually only a few are damaged and yields are not affected.

PREVENTION AND CONTROL There is no way to stop bees robbing nectar.

See also

Bud drop (page 84), Frost and wind damage (page 85), Pollen beetle (page 85).

Apple sucker

Blossom wilt

Nectar-robbing bee

Apple scab

Fruit problems

Apple and pear scab

This fungal disease affects the leaves and twigs of apples and pears but is most evident on the fruit. These are covered with thick, corky patches of rough tissue that crack and allow the flesh to rot. Sometimes the fruit is tiny and misshapen.
PLANTS AFFECTED Apples and pears; also ornamental crab apples (*Malus*).
HOW BAD IS IT? Some fruit may still be edible with judicious peeling. The fungus can overwinter in affected trees and may weaken them.
PREVENTION AND CONTROL Rake up and dispose of leaves in the autumn. Prune trees carefully to remove overcrowded branches and those that are diseased. As a last resort, use a fungicide. There are many apple varieties resistant to scab, including 'Discovery' and 'Red Devil'; resistant pears include 'Beurre Hardy' and 'Jargonelle'.

Apple bitter pit

Apple bitter pit

Bitter pit is caused by a nutrient deficiency, and symptoms may appear only when the apples are picked and in storage. The fruits will have many tiny, brown, indented spots all over their skin. When the apple is peeled, there is a corresponding small brown area of flesh underneath each spot. The apples taste bitter even when these spots are removed.
PLANTS AFFECTED Apples; it is worse on large fruit and those from a heavy crop.
HOW BAD IS IT? This is an unwelcome condition, but treatment will prevent reoccurrence in following years.
PREVENTION AND CONTROL Bitter pit is a symptom of calcium deficiency, which is normally due to dry soil preventing the tree from obtaining what it needs. Water well and mulch to retain moisture. Feed

with a balanced fertilizer, but do not overfeed, since this can prevent calcium uptake. Spray the fruits with calcium nitrate several times as they are developing.

Apple capsid bug

The apple capsid is a small, bright green insect that feeds on young fruit and shoot-tips in summer. As the leaves develop they may become distorted, tattered and holey, and the mature fruit is also affected, with rough, green or yellow-brown bumps on the surface.
PLANTS AFFECTED Apples.
HOW BAD IS IT? The taste of the fruit is not spoiled and the leaf damage is not usually extensive, so light infestations can be ignored.
PREVENTION AND CONTROL If you have had heavy attacks in previous years, spray with pyrethrum as the petals fall from around the developing fruit.

Apple fruit split

Lack of water while they are developing can make young apples split, particularly around the stalk end. Splits are usually shallow and often heal over if the fruit is still growing, leaving a corky scar. Later in the season, splits may allow rots to set in.
PLANTS AFFECTED Apples.
HOW BAD IS IT? If the splits are slight, eating quality will not be affected, but storage will be; splits that develop late in the season are more serious.
PREVENTION AND CONTROL Splitting is common in dry summers where rain comes in rare but heavy downpours. Ensure that your trees get enough water throughout the growing season, and mulch around the base in spring to retain moisture.

Apple fruit split

Bean anthracnose

This fungal disease produces brown or reddish sunken spots on the pods and stems of beans. The leaves are also usually affected, showing red in the veins, and turning brown and dying. Anthracnose is worse during wet weather, which may make the marks on the pods become pink and slimy.

PLANTS AFFECTED Dwarf French beans and runner beans.

HOW BAD IS IT? The crop of affected plants will be ruined. Dig them up and destroy them to avoid spread; they will eventually die anyway.

PREVENTION AND CONTROL Clear away plant debris at the end of the growing season to prevent overwintering. Practise crop rotation. Anthracnose can be carried in seed, so don't save your own bean seeds if you have had an infection. Grow varieties that have some resistance, such as 'Aramis'.

Bitter cucumbers

It is such a disappointment to bite into a fresh, succulent cucumber and find it tastes rather unpleasant. There are two causes: one reason is sudden changes in growing conditions, such as drops in temperature, the other is pollination of the flowers (pollinated fruit is often club-shaped).

PLANTS AFFECTED Cucumbers.

HOW BAD IS IT? Early in the fruiting season the problem is easily addressed, although fruit that has formed on the vine may already be spoiled.

PREVENTION AND CONTROL Remove the male flowers, which have no embryo fruit (see the upper flower in the illustration) before they open. Subsequent fruit should be edible. Grow cucumbers that produce only female flowers, such as 'Carmen', 'Tiffany' and 'Flamingo'. If the cause is fluctuating conditions, grow your plants under cover. A cloche or a fleece placed over the plants at night and on cold days will reduce temperature variation. Don't overfeed, and water regularly.

Brown curd of cauliflowers

Cauliflowers are difficult to grow well, and this unattractive condition occurs when the plants are short of boron (see page 25). The curds discolour to brown and are usually small and poorly developed. The main stem and leaf-stalks may be rough.

PLANTS AFFECTED Cauliflowers.

HOW BAD IS IT? Brown curds are not tasty, so the crop may be spoiled. Fixing the cause will prevent further problems.

PREVENTION AND CONTROL Prepare the ground well before planting (see pages 20 and 24). Curds exposed to bad weather may also discolour, so bend the leaves over them as they develop. Pay attention to feeding, watering and weeding.

Brown rot

Brown rot starts as soft areas in the skin. These turn brown and eventually develop cream-coloured mould spots, often in concentric rings. The flesh beneath rots, and soon the whole fruit is rotten. Birds, codling moths (see page 102) or other insects damage fruit and make it prone to rot, as do scab infections or cracks.

PLANTS AFFECTED Many fruit, particularly apples.

HOW BAD IS IT? Rot spreads fast, so pick and destroy diseased fruit promptly.

PREVENTION AND CONTROL Pick up fallen fruit from around trees. Prune out withered fruitlets. Make sure plants are properly fed, watered and pruned. Do not store affected fruit, and check stored fruit very regularly.

Bean anthracnose

Bitter cucumber

Brown rot

Codling moth

Pea moth

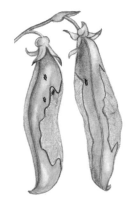

Pea thrips

Codling moth

The white caterpillars of this moth tunnel into tree fruit in mid- or late summer and feed there until they are mature, often tunnelling back out at the base in autumn.
PLANTS AFFECTED Apples and pears.
HOW BAD IS IT? The fruit will be ruined and much of the crop can be affected.
PREVENTION AND CONTROL
Pheromone traps (*see* page 27) alert you to the problem and may reduce numbers. The biological control *Steinernema carpocapsae* (*see* page 27) may help where attacks are heavy. As a last resort, spray with a pesticide approved for crops twice in early summer when you find adult moths in pheromone traps.

Fruit drop

Fruits fall off a healthy tree before they are ripe or just as they reach maturity. Some trees, particularly apples, routinely shed excess fruit, as do trees that are struggling in less-than-perfect growing conditions. Windy weather may also be a cause, as can pest attack (*see* sawflies page 72), so check fallen fruit for insect damage.
PLANTS AFFECTED Tree fruit, such as apples, pears (*see also* Pear midge, opposite) and plums.
HOW BAD IS IT? Fruit drop is rarely anything to worry about.
PREVENTION AND CONTROL Improve growing conditions as much as possible. Stake young trees, and water and feed well. Prune regularly and mulch in spring. Thin heavy crops in early summer, and harvest before autumn storms.

Fruit failure

If a healthy tree produces flowers but there are no signs of any fruit when the petals drop, the flowers have not been pollinated. This might be because of a lack of suitable pollen or because cold weather has damaged the flowers.
PLANTS AFFECTED Apples, cherries, kiwi fruit, pears, peaches, nectarines, plums.
HOW BAD IS IT? Rectify the cause and it should not reoccur.
PREVENTION AND CONTROL Many fruit trees need pollen from a different variety of the same species; female kiwi plants need a male plant. Make sure your tree's needs are met: you may need to plant a partner. Protect early flowers from frost and wind damage.

Pea moth

The pea moth lays eggs on flowering pea plants between early and late summer. When they hatch, the tiny, dark-spotted, white caterpillars burrow into the pods to eat the young peas. The pods look fine from the outside; it is only when they are harvested that the damage is revealed.
PLANTS AFFECTED Peas.
HOW BAD IS IT? Usually only one or two peas per pod are spoiled.
PREVENTION AND CONTROL Sow early varieties, such as 'Feltham First' or 'Douce Provençe', which flower before the moth is active, or mangetout or sugar snaps, which are eaten when too small to be damaged. Protect plants with horticultural fleece and practise crop rotation, because the larvae overwinter in the soil. As a last resort, spray with a suitable pesticide about seven days after the pea flowers open.

Pea thrips

In a hot, dry summer, thrips (*see* page 73) can cause extensive damage in the vegetable garden. Pea thrips eat the skin of pea pods, distorting the pods and creating extensive silvery patches of dried tissue.

PLANTS AFFECTED Peas.

HOW BAD IS IT? Yields can be badly affected, since often only two or three peas may develop in each pod, and the crop may be less succulent and tasty.

PREVENTION AND CONTROL Keep plants well watered in dry weather. Spray with pyrethrum or plant and fish oils as soon as you see damage or, as a last resort, a chemical pesticide approved for crops.

Peach split stone

This is a physiological problem: the stone splits inside the ripening peach and the skin around the stalk tears, allowing fungal diseases to enter the fruit and cause rot.

PLANTS AFFECTED Peaches.

HOW BAD IS IT? Affected peaches are often misshapen and inedible.

PREVENTION AND CONTROL The problem may be caused by erratic water supply or poor pollination. Water regularly, particularly in dry weather, and mulch in spring. Consider pollinating flowers yourself, using a small watercolour brush.

Pear midge

The minute, maggot-like larvae of the pear midge infest the pear fruitlets, feeding on the flesh and eventually turning the skin black. The fruit stop developing and fall from the tree as early as late spring.

PLANTS AFFECTED Pears.

HOW BAD IS IT? A heavy infestation can reduce yields to almost nothing.

PREVENTION AND CONTROL Pick off infested fruitlets as soon as you see signs of attack. This can only really be done on small trees and will reduce numbers, but does not save your harvest. As a last resort, spray with a suitable chemical pesticide in spring, when the flower buds are just beginning to show the white of the petals.

Pear stony pit virus

This virus disease causes pears to develop many tiny, gritty granules inside the flesh. The fruit often remains small and is misshapen by these pits, and eating it is unpleasant. The leaves may also be sparse and yellow along the smaller veins.

PLANTS AFFECTED Pears – old trees are most commonly affected. 'Anjou' and 'Doyenné du Comice' are among cultivars known to be susceptible.

HOW BAD IS IT? Usually the problem is limited to a branch or two; the rest of the fruit is edible.

PREVENTION AND CONTROL There are no treatments. Removing affected branches does not help, since the virus simply appears elsewhere. Where much of the fruit is affected, plant new trees and avoid susceptible cultivars.

Raspberry beetle

The grey-brown raspberry beetle lays its eggs on the flowers of cane fruit in early to midsummer. When the off-white larvae hatch they feed on the base of the berries, later entering them and feeding at the core.

PLANTS AFFECTED Cane fruit including blackberries, loganberries, raspberries and tayberries. Late-fruiting autumn raspberries are unaffected.

HOW BAD IS IT? The larvae-infested fruit are unappetizing, and the damage can allow fungal infections to take hold.

PREVENTION AND CONTROL Traps consisting of white, petal-like panels that lure the raspberry beetle away from the flowers are available, but expensive if you have only a few canes. Sticky traps may reduce numbers. Spray tiny raspberry fruitlets with pyrethrum-based insecticide twice, with an interval of two weeks. Spray blackberries when the flowers open and other berries when the petals fall.

Pear midge

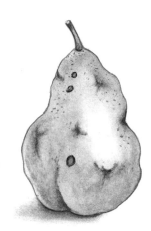

Pear stony pit virus

Raspberry beetle

Apple sawfly

Plum sawfly

Strawberry grey mould

Sawflies

Like other sawflies, the adult forms of apple and plum sawflies (*Hoplocampa testudinea* and *H. flava*) are more or less harmless. It is their larvae that do the damage, in these cases to fruit. The sawflies lay their eggs in the tiny fruitlets when the trees are still in bloom. The larvae hatch and feed in the young fruit, filling their lairs with dark excrement. They cause early dropping of the fruit.

PLANTS AFFECTED Apples and plums, and in particular the plum varieties 'Czar' and 'Victoria'.

HOW BAD IS IT? Usually not all of the fruits on the tree are affected. With apples, the larvae may die early, leaving a fruit that has a scar on the skin but is otherwise edible.

PREVENTION AND CONTROL On small trees, pick off affected fruitlets. Do not leave fallen fruit on the ground, as this will allow the larvae to get into the soil, where they pupate and complete their life cycle. As a preventative measure where sawflies have been a regular pest in previous years, spray with pyrethrum or a chemical pesticide approved for crops as the petals drop.

Shanking of grapes

This is thought to be a physiological disorder caused by poor growing conditions. Some of the fruit in a bunch of grapes stop developing normally; they don't change colour or ripen and may shrivel and become raisin-like.

PLANTS AFFECTED Grapes.

HOW BAD IS IT? The rest of the fruit in the bunch is usually fine, but the affected grapes are inedible.

PREVENTION AND CONTROL Pay great attention to feeding and watering your grape vines. Do not over- or underwater, since both of these may be a cause of shanking. Feed regularly, applying a foliar feed to boost grape production. Check developing fruit and remove any shanked grapes from the bunches as soon as you see them.

Strawberry black eye

On a healthy strawberry plant, the centre of the flower develops a dark centre, and the flowers do not develop into fruit. The cause is frost damage to the flowers.

PLANTS AFFECTED Strawberries.

HOW BAD IS IT? Crops are reduced for the year, but addressing the cause will prevent reoccurrence.

PREVENTION AND CONTROL Cover early-flowering strawberries with cloches or horticultural fleece until the risk of frost is over. If flowers are frosted, pinch them out: later flowers will still produce fruit.

Strawberry grey mould

The fungal disease *Botrytis cinerea* (*see* Grey mould, page 68) enters the embryonic fruit before the flower petals fall. It remains dormant as the fruit develops, but when weather conditions are suitably damp it will infect them and cause pale brown rotting patches, which then produce a grey, fluffy mould.

PLANTS AFFECTED Strawberries.

HOW BAD IS IT? Affected fruit is inedible and spores spread readily.

PREVENTION AND CONTROL Botrytis is always present on dead and living plant material all over the garden, so it is impossible to exclude entirely. Remove any dead or dying leaves and damaged fruit from around strawberry plants. Place protective strawberry mats under fruit to keep them dry and prevent rain splash from the ground.

Strawberry seed beetle

For much of the year, strawberry seed beetles eat weed seeds, so they are helpful to gardeners. However, when strawberries are about they like to graze the seeds from the fruit, leaving small brown scars. The beetles are black and very fast-moving, and they feed mostly at night, so you are unlikely to see them.

PLANTS AFFECTED Strawberries.

HOW BAD IS IT? Badly eaten fruit will be inedible, particularly as the damage may encourage rots to develop.

PREVENTION AND CONTROL There are few satisfactory controls. Jam jars sunk into the ground will capture a few, but they will also trap useful beetles, so remember to check them regularly. Keeping your strawberry patch weed-free will reduce weed seeds and therefore the numbers of seed beetles.

Sweetcorn smut

This fungal disease of sweetcorn can infect the stems and leaves as well as the cobs. Gall-like growths may appear on the leaves and stalks, while the individual kernels on a cob will be unnaturally large and deformed – the cob is clearly distorted under its protective sheath. The affected kernels are usually greyish and soon burst open to release large quantities of spores. In rainy weather, these leave black streaks down the stems of plants. Normal and infected cobs can develop on the same plant.

PLANTS AFFECTED Sweetcorn.

HOW BAD IS IT? Infected cobs look unappetizing, but if they are harvested before the spores develop, the galls are edible, although perhaps not to everyone's taste. In Mexico, they are deliberately cultivated as a delicacy. Not all plants develop the disease.

PREVENTION AND CONTROL Remove any infected plants as soon as you see them. Do not allow the spore-laden kernels to burst, and avoid growing sweetcorn in the infected spot for five years. Grow resistant varieties, including 'Ambrosia' and 'Tendersweet'.

Wasps

Wasps are not just unwelcome visitors at garden parties; in late summer, they like to eat fresh fruit and easily make a meal of them, boring holes into them and feeding on the flesh. Where fruit is damaged, several wasps may be found inside. They make large holes that then encourage other pests, such as slugs.

PLANTS AFFECTED Many, including apples, figs, grapes, nectarines, peaches, pears and plums.

HOW BAD IS IT? Softer fruit, such as grapes and plums, are quickly ruined, while larger apples and pears may be salvaged for immediate eating if you cut out the damaged areas. It is rare for every fruit on a plant to be attacked.

PREVENTION AND CONTROL Pick fruit as soon as it is ripe and regularly remove fallen fruit from around the base of trees, since these will encourage wasps. You can make wasp traps using a jam jar. Dissolve a teaspoonful of jam in a cup of warm water and pour this into the jar. Put a circle of paper over the top and secure it with an elastic band, then make a hole just large enough for a wasp to crawl through in the centre of the paper. Secure string or wire tightly around the top of the jar and hang the trap in or near the affected trees and empty it regularly.

See also

Bird damage (page 99), Buckeye rot (page 106), Caterpillars (page 107).

Strawberry seed beetle

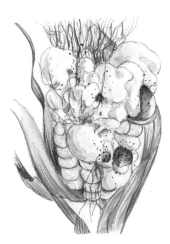

Sweetcorn smut

Wasp

Blight

Blossom end rot

Buckeye rot

Tomato problems

Blight

Tomato blight is caused by the fungus *Phytophthora infestans*. The leaves develop brown patches that soon start to curl and dry. Brown marks also appear on the stems and fruit. On fruit the patches are sunken and the fruit soon rots. Plants outdoors are more likely to be infected than those under cover, which are protected from the drifting spores.

PLANTS AFFECTED Tomatoes and potatoes (*see* page 96).

HOW BAD IS IT? Plants usually die, but not as fast as potatoes. Crops are spoiled.

PREVENTION AND CONTROL Once plants are infected, there is no cure for this disease. If your tomatoes regularly suffer from blight, preventative spraying with a suitable fungicide is the only control. Spray as soon as tomatoes start to set. The blight is more common in wet seasons, so spray according to the weather conditions if you prefer to keep spraying to a minimum.

Blossom end rot

Blossom end rot is caused by calcium deficiency. A sunken, rotten area develops where the petals fell off, opposite the stalk. Affected patches are brown and tough.

PLANTS AFFECTED Tomatoes, but rarely small-fruited varieties; sweet peppers.

HOW BAD IS IT? Usually not all the fruits on a truss are affected, so you should still get a reasonable crop.

PREVENTION AND CONTROL This condition is more common on container-grown plants that have received inadequate water, preventing calcium uptake from the soil. Make sure your plants are watered regularly. Use larger containers that don't dry out so quickly or plant your tomatoes into the ground.

Blotchy ripening

This phenomenon occurs most frequently in tomatoes that are grown under cover and is thought to be caused by high temperatures combined with a lack of potash. The fruit ripens in part, but retains yellow or green areas where the flesh remains hard. The surface of the affected areas may look uneven and lumpy. Greenback (*see* opposite) is similar.

PLANTS AFFECTED Tomatoes.

HOW BAD IS IT? Usually fruit on the lower trusses are spoiled, but not all are affected, so you will still get a crop.

PREVENTION AND CONTROL Shade greenhouses to avoid excessive heat and scorching. Increase ventilation and damp down several times a day. Water plants well and regularly. Feed with tomato fertilizer, which is high in potash.

Buckeye rot

Buckeye rot is caused by a phytophthora fungus (*P. parasitica*). It starts as a brown spot on unripe fruit that soon develops encircling concentric bands of rot, looking somewhat like a target. In wet weather, white, fluffy fungal growths may appear and, occasionally, the stems and roots can suffer damage too.

PLANTS AFFECTED Aubergines, peppers and tomatoes.

HOW BAD IS IT? Not all fruit will be spoiled. Fruit nearer the ground is more usually affected, because the fungus is spread by water splashing soil and spores up onto the fruit.

PREVENTION AND CONTROL This disease is more common under cover and flourishes in warm, damp conditions, so increase air circulation around your plants. Support fruit trusses, holding them well up away from the ground. Consider placing protective mats or sheets of newspaper around the bases of plants, or water carefully to avoid splashing.

Caterpillars

The dark brown tomato moth (*Lacanobia oleracea*) is the most common cause of problems. It lays its eggs on tomato leaves and the young caterpillars feed in groups, grazing the lower leaf tissue away so that the upper leaf surface dries to white. Later they move onto the fruit and tunnel into it. Tomato moth caterpillars are brown or green, with a pale line along both flanks and many tiny dots.

PLANTS AFFECTED Tomatoes; sometimes also aubergines.

HOW BAD IS IT? Fruit that has been bored into will be inedible. Caterpillars can wreak great destruction and must be stopped if your crop is to be saved.

PREVENTION AND CONTROL Pick off the caterpillars as soon as you see them. Remove any leaves that are carrying eggs. Use pyrethrum spray to reduce numbers if necessary. As a last resort, use a pesticide approved for crops.

Dry set

Tomatoes flower as normal and the fruitlets begin to grow but stop when they are still tiny, often smaller than a pea. This usually occurs when the flowers are produced during hot, dry weather which prevents proper pollination. Dry set may also be caused by viruses (*see* page 108).

PLANTS AFFECTED Tomatoes.

HOW BAD IS IT? Dry set tomatoes turn brown and dry. Usually not all tomatoes on a plant are affected.

PREVENTION AND CONTROL During dry weather, mist plants in the early

morning, before the sun is too strong. Give trusses a gentle shake to encourage the pollen to fall.

Ghost spot

Unripe tomatoes may develop very faint, pale green or sometimes yellow spots or rings. While the rest of the fruit ripens, these spots usually darken to deeper yellow or faint orange. They are caused by the grey mould fungus *Botrytis cinerea* (*see* page 68).

PLANTS AFFECTED Tomatoes.

HOW BAD IS IT? The spotted tomatoes are edible and the spots do not spoil the taste; not all fruit on a truss will be affected.

PREVENTION AND CONTROL Grey mould spores are everywhere in gardens, greenhouses and polytunnels. In this instance they are not harmful, but they can cause more serious problems, so limit their spread by clearing up plant debris. Increase ventilation under cover.

Greenback

Tomatoes fail to ripen around the stalk end. The skin stays green or yellow, often becoming thick and leathery in a circle around the stalk. It is thought that the main cause is high light levels under cover, but deficiency in potassium and phosphorus may increase its occurrence.

PLANTS AFFECTED Tomatoes.

HOW BAD IS IT? Fruits that have greenback are not edible, but not all fruits on a plant will be affected.

PREVENTION AND CONTROL Shade greenhouses early on, before plants flower and set fruit. Increase ventilation on hot days and damp down two or three times a day. Water plentifully and feed regularly. Avoid excessive feeding, since this brings its own problems. Many modern F1 hybrids are resistant to greenback.

Tomato moth caterpillar

Ghost spot

Greenback

Tomato leaf mould

Fern leaf virus

Spotted wilt virus

Hollow fruit

Tomatoes develop and ripen but contain no seeds or juice. Possible causes include weedkiller damage, virus infections, poor pollination and poor growing conditions.
PLANTS AFFECTED Tomatoes.
HOW BAD IS IT? The fruits are edible, but are not as juicy or tasty as usual.
PREVENTION AND CONTROL Feed and water regularly. Plant tomatoes in warm, sheltered spots or under cover to minimize temperature fluctuations. Shake the flowering trusses to assist pollination. Do not use weedkillers near tomatoes.

Splitting fruit

The skins of tomatoes split just as the fruit reaches maturity. The splits may dry and simply look unappetizing or they may remain wet, allowing fungal diseases into the flesh, which will develop grey mould (*see* page 68) and become inedible.
PLANTS AFFECTED Tomatoes; some thin-skinned, small-fruited varieties are particularly susceptible.
HOW BAD IS IT? Usually not all fruit on a truss are affected.
PREVENTION AND CONTROL Splits are caused by fluctuations in water supply or temperature. Provide ventilation and shade under cover and ensure plants get regular and adequate water.

Tomato leaf mould

Tomatoes under cover develop yellow patches on the upper leaf surface, with matching grey or purple fuzzy areas on the underside. They eventually dry, become brown and die. Grey mould (*see* page 68) may also invade infected plants.
PLANTS AFFECTED Tomatoes.
HOW BAD IS IT? Plants suffer reduced vigour and therefore lower yields.

PREVENTION AND CONTROL Improve air circulation by increasing spacing and removing some leaves. Open doors and vents on warm, damp days. Clear away plant debris; burn infected plants at the end of the growing season.

Viruses

Tomato viruses include fern leaf, spotted wilt, and cucumber and tobacco mosaic viruses. Among the symptoms are small, distorted leaves or patterning on the leaves. Plants are usually stunted and may suffer dry set (*see* page 107). Fruit is often discoloured or fails to ripen normally. Weedkillers can cause similar symptoms.
PLANTS AFFECTED Tomatoes.
HOW BAD IS IT? Plants rarely develop healthy fruit and should be destroyed to prevent spread to other healthy tomatoes.
PREVENTION AND CONTROL Dig up and destroy affected plants. Viruses are easily spread, so wash your hands after handling infected plants and keep your tools, such as secateurs, scrupulously clean. Keep sap-sucking pests, such as aphids (*see* page 90) and thrips (*see* page 73), under control, because they spread viruses through their feeding activities. Some cultivars, including 'Estrella' and 'Shirley', are resistant to tobacco mosaic virus. Make sure weedkillers are not used near tomato plants – they can travel quite a distance on the breeze.

See also

Aphids (page 90), Colorado beetle (page 93), Cutworms (page 82), Damping off (page 81), Downy mildew (page 66), Fungal wilts (page 67), Grey mould (page 68), Mealy bug (page 70), Potato cyst eelworm (page 96), Powdery mildew (page 70), Red spider mite (page 71), Root knot eelworm (page 113), Whitefly (page 74).

Root and plant base problems

Bacterial soft rot

This rotting disease of roots, tubers and rhizomes at first produces patches of discoloration on the affected area. These quickly spread, causing softening and sinking of the underlying tissues. Fruit may also be affected.

PLANTS AFFECTED Most plants.

HOW BAD IS IT? Because of the speed of spread and the fact that the damage is initially out of sight, it is often fatal; if it is caught early enough, parts of the plant may be salvaged.

PREVENTION AND CONTROL Avoid damage to roots, since bacteria often gain entry via wounds. If the infection takes hold, you may be able to rescue plants by removing all the damaged tissue, cutting back into healthy areas. Disinfect your tools as you work to avoid transferring the infection to other plants.

Bean seed fly

The white, maggotty larvae of the bean seed fly (*Delia platura*) attack seeds just as they begin to germinate. If the seedlings get above the soil surface, they will have damaged stems and leaves. The bean seed fly looks like a housefly.

PLANTS AFFECTED French beans and runner beans and some other slow-to-germinate seed.

HOW BAD IS IT? If the seedlings manage to appear above the soil, they usually survive, but they will need careful looking after at first.

PREVENTION AND CONTROL Start seeds in pots and plant them out when the weather conditions are perfect for rapid growth. Avoid adding fresh compost to the soil in spring, since this will attract the fly; dig it in during the autumn instead.

Cabbage root fly

This pest lays eggs at the base of plants in the cabbage family. When the larvae hatch out, they migrate into the soil and eat all the fine roots, leaving just the central stem. They may also tunnel into root crops.

PLANTS AFFECTED Members of the cabbage (*Brassica*) family, including turnips and radishes; related ornamentals, such as stocks and wallflowers.

HOW BAD IS IT? Seedlings or transplants are more likely to suffer and die than larger plants, which can fend off attacks.

PREVENTION AND CONTROL Place mats around the base of plants to stop the larvae from reaching the roots. Mats can be made from cardboard, old carpeting or any other robust material. Cover seed beds and transplants with horticultural fleece to prevent the fly reaching the soil.

Carrot fly

Brown-stained tunnels around the top and sides of root crops are signs of infestation by carrot root fly larvae. These off-white maggots feed just under the skin and the damage is vulnerable to rotting diseases.

PLANTS AFFECTED Carrots, celery and parsnips; sometimes parsley roots.

HOW BAD IS IT? Less badly damaged roots may still be edible after careful peeling, but the tunnelling makes them unappetizing. Such roots should not be stored, since they are very likely to rot.

PREVENTION AND CONTROL After sowing, cover seed beds with horticultural fleece to prevent the fly reaching them to lay her eggs. Avoid thinning seedlings since the distinctive smell of young carrots attracts the fly. Grow resistant carrot varieties such as 'Flyaway' and 'Resistafly'. (*See* also Companion planting, page 11.)

Bacterial soft rot

Cabbage root fly

Carrot fly

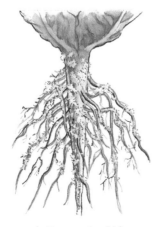

Club root

Fanging

Lettuce root aphid

Carrot green top

The tops of carrots turn green around the leaf bases and the green colouring may extend down around the 'shoulders'. This is caused by sunlight reaching the roots.
PLANTS AFFECTED Carrots.
HOW BAD IS IT? The eating and keeping quality is unaffected.
PREVENTION AND CONTROL Keep checking on your carrots as they grow and earth up as necessary to prevent the tops being exposed to the sun.

Club root

Leaves and stems of plants suffering from this fungal disease become pale green or tinged with purple or pink, and the plant wilts very easily in dry weather. Inspection of the roots reveals large, smelly swellings and lumps.
PLANTS AFFECTED Members of the cabbage (*Brassica*) family, and related ornamentals such as aubrieta, candytuft (*Iberis*), stocks (*Matthiola*) and wallflowers (*Cheiranthus* and *Erysimum*).
HOW BAD IS IT? Plants are stunted; they do not crop well and may die.
PREVENTION AND CONTROL Once present, club root cannot be eradicated, but its effects may be reduced. Grow brassicas to a larger size before planting out: pot them up into 9cm (3½in) pots. Add lime to the soil and take measures to improve drainage. Weed regularly, since some weeds can harbour infection. Grow resistant varieties, such as cabbage 'Kilaton', calabrese 'Trixie', cauliflower 'Clapton' and kale 'Tall Green Curled'.

Fanging

Instead of single thick roots, crops produce divided roots with two or more main growths and sometimes smaller outgrowths. They may also be twisted and misshapen in other ways. The most common causes are stones in the ground or the recent addition of manure or compost to the soil.
PLANTS AFFECTED Beetroots, carrots and parsnips.
HOW BAD IS IT? Although it is unsightly and makes peeling more time-consuming, fanging has no effect on edibility.
PREVENTION AND CONTROL Dig soil well and deeply; where possible remove large stones. Allow a year (grow another crop in the site) between adding compost or manure to a plot and growing root vegetables there.

Lettuce root aphid

This soil-dwelling pest feeds on the roots of lettuces. Plants first show symptoms of infestation by wilting in dry weather and failing to grow as expected. When you dig up the plants, you see white powder covering the roots and groups of pale yellow aphids. The aphids are most active during mid- and late summer.
PLANTS AFFECTED Lettuces.
HOW BAD IS IT? Lettuces grow slowly, if at all. They are best disposed of.
PREVENTION AND CONTROL Practise crop rotation to prevent build-up of soil pests. Use horticultural fleece to prevent the aphids reaching the roots and water plants well to enable them to withstand any infestations. Grow lettuces that show resistance, such as 'Avondefiance', 'Lakeland' and 'Little Gem'.

Onion bull neck

Onions sometimes produce rather thick necks, without the usual clear distinction between the bulb and the leaves. This is a physiological disorder that may be caused by planting onion seed too deeply. It also occurs when onions are overfed.

PLANTS AFFECTED Onions.

HOW BAD IS IT? The onions are still edible but they will not store well, since the wide neck opening leaves them vulnerable to fungal and bacterial disease.

PREVENTION AND CONTROL Make sure you plant seed at the recommended depth, or use onion sets. Avoid planting onions in recently manured soil; add manure in the autumn before planting in spring. Feed with liquid tomato fertilizer, which is rich in potassium to promote strong root growth, but does not contain too much nitrogen.

Onion fly

Onion bulbs and roots may be attacked by the white, maggoty larvae of the onion fly (*Delia antiqua*), which looks like a housefly. The problem usually becomes evident in early summer, when plants that seem to have been growing well suddenly collapse. A second generation attacks in late summer. Rots get into the bulbs through the larval damage.

PLANTS AFFECTED Usually onions, but also garlic, leeks and shallots.

HOW BAD IS IT? Affected bulbs will die.

PREVENTION AND CONTROL Dig up and destroy infested bulbs. Dig through the surrounding soil to expose as many maggots as possible – let the birds finish them off. Grow onions from sets, rather than seed, since these are less vulnerable. Cover onion beds with horticultural fleece to prevent the flies reaching their target.

Onion rot

There are two types of rot that affect onions: white rot and neck rot. White rot produces a white fungal growth around

the bulb base during growth, killing the plants. Neck rot is caused by *Botrytis allii*. This appears in storage and makes the bulb soft and brown and produces a grey, fuzzy growth. Both types of rot go on to produce tiny, black, seed-like sclerotia (dormant fungal fruit bodies).

PLANTS AFFECTED Onions.

HOW BAD IS IT? Both ruin the crop.

PREVENTION AND CONTROL Practise crop rotation, since this prevents the build-up of fungal infection in the first place. Dig up and destroy any onions suffering from white rot and do not grow onions or related plants, such as leeks, in the same spot for eight years. Buy onion sets from reputable sources. Water adequately, but do not feed excessively. Red and yellow bulbs are less likely to succumb to neck rot. Do not bend stems over at harvest time, but allow this to happen naturally; dry onions for storage with the stems pointing downwards.

Parsnip canker

Two different fungal infections of parsnips produce red-brown or black cankers on the roots, usually around the top. The infection may spread via leaf spots (*see* page 69) or through the finer feeding roots.

PLANTS AFFECTED Parsnips; also beetroot, carrots and celery.

HOW BAD IS IT? Some roots may be edible. Badly infected roots soon rot.

PREVENTION AND CONTROL Practise crop rotation. Add lime to achieve a pH of 6.5 (*see* pages 14–15); improve drainage. Reduce spacing to produce smaller roots, which are less vulnerable. Cover seed beds with horticultural fleece to prevent carrot fly damage. Once the foliage is quite thick, earth up to cover any visible part of the roots. Take care not to damage roots during hoeing. Grow resistant varieties, such as 'Avonresister' and 'Cobham Improved Marrow'.

Onion fly

Onion rot

Parsnip canker

Potato gangrene

This fungal disease infects potatoes after they have been harvested. It appears as well-defined, pitted areas, sometimes surrounded by slightly wrinkled skin. The tubers begin to rot, becoming wet and pale pink, then grey-brown or blackish.

PLANTS AFFECTED Potatoes.

HOW BAD IS IT? Affected tubers cannot be stored. The disease may spread to previously healthy tubers.

PREVENTION AND CONTROL Damaged areas on lifted potatoes are most vulnerable to gangrene. Take care when harvesting. Keep damaged potatoes to one side and use them first; check all stored potatoes regularly and discard any showing signs of decay.

Potato gangrene

Potato hollow heart

This is a physiological condition that affects large tubers. The potato has all the appearance of being completely normal, but when cut open its centre is hollow, often split into fissures. The flesh surrounding the hollow area is usually rough and dark.

PLANTS AFFECTED Potatoes.

HOW BAD IS IT? Although probably still edible, hollow potatoes are unappetizing and best discarded. Usually only a few tubers in a crop will be affected.

PREVENTION AND CONTROL Erratic water supply and testing weather conditions when the tubers are in full growth are the usual causes of hollow heart. For example, periods of overwatering followed by drought, or spells of dry weather during which plants are given varying amounts of water may both produce the problem, as may overfeeding. Water regularly and plentifully, but not too heavily, especially when the weather is dry and hot.

Potato powdery scab

Potato scab

Potato powdery scab

Powdery scab is a fungal disease of potato tubers, producing round patches of warty, blistered tissue. These scabs form during growth and if they reach maturity before the potatoes are harvested, they burst and release their spores into the soil. Sometimes the tubers produce large, unsightly growths.

PLANTS AFFECTED Potatoes.

HOW BAD IS IT? Infected potatoes are inedible. This disease is not very common, but if it is present in the soil it may spoil a proportion of your crop.

PREVENTION AND CONTROL Practise crop rotation, since this disease is more likely to occur on ground that is regularly used for potatoes. Improve drainage. If your potatoes get powdery scab, do not grow them on the same site for at least three years. Grow resistant varieties, such as 'Desirée' and 'Santé'. Avoid 'Pentland Crown', which is very susceptible.

Potato scab

Often called common scab, this fungal disease of potatoes is one that most growers will come across. The scabs are wide, flat areas of rough skin that are pitted with shallow, angular splits. The scabs are only skin deep, and the flesh beneath them is not spoiled.

PLANTS AFFECTED Potatoes, beetroot, radishes, swedes, turnips.

HOW BAD IS IT? Apart from the fact that the scabs are unsightly, the only inconvenience is the additional peeling work required. Tubers can be stored without a problem.

PREVENTION AND CONTROL The disease is most prevalent on dry, sandy and alkaline soils, so do not lime your soil when planting potatoes but do incorporate plenty of organic matter.

Consider adding sulphate of ammonia to increase acidity. Water potatoes during dry weather. Resistant varieties include 'Arran Pilot', 'Nadine' and 'Wilja', while 'Desirée' and 'Maris Piper' are susceptible.

Root knot eelworm

In Britain, these microscopic creatures are most likely to be a problem for crops growing in greenhouses, where they burrow into roots and cause gall-like growths. Above ground, the main symptoms are poor growth and pale leaf colouring, because the galls restrict movement of food and water around the plant. Plants outdoors growing on very light, sandy soil may also occasionally have problems with these eelworms.

PLANTS AFFECTED Cucumber, lettuce and tomato; greenhouse ornamentals may also be affected.

HOW BAD IS IT? Plants will not thrive, and eventually die. They should be dug up and discarded as soon as the problem is identified to prevent its spread.

PREVENTION AND CONTROL In greenhouses, remove affected plants. If the eelworms are present in greenhouse borders, consider replacing as much of this soil as possible to reduce the problem. Alternatively, grow plants in containers.

Wart disease of potatoes

You are unlikely to come across this fungal disease of potatoes now, but it was once serious and common enough to be notifiable. It causes knobbly, warty outgrowths on the tubers, which may otherwise look quite normal; at first off-white, the growths soon turn black and have been likened to cauliflowers. The disease may be barely visible on the potatoes when they are lifted, but

continues to develop in storage, sometimes covering the whole tuber. (*See also* Potato powdery scab, opposite.)

PLANTS AFFECTED Potatoes.

HOW BAD IS IT? Potatoes that are only slightly affected may still be eaten, but they will soon rot in storage.

PREVENTION AND CONTROL Most commonly grown potatoes are resistant to the fungus, but exceptions include 'King Edward' and 'Sharpe's Express'. This fungus remains active in the soil for 30 years, so potatoes cannot be grown in that site again. If you suspect wart disease in your plants, notify your local authority.

Wireworm

The larvae of click beetles are long, thin, orange- or yellow-brown worms with three pairs of legs. They burrow into root crops, making small, round holes. Once inside, they tunnel extensively. They may also eat the stems of seedlings just below the soil surface. Adult beetles cause no damage.

PLANTS AFFECTED French beans, lettuces, onions, strawberries; roots of carrots and potatoes; seedlings of almost any plant.

HOW BAD IS IT? Crops may be ruined and plants can be stunted or killed.

PREVENTION AND CONTROL Wireworms are most often found where a new bed or vegetable patch is created from grassland. Their numbers reduce over two or three years of regular cultivation, and they usually stop being a real problem. Harvest root crops early to limit damage and raise seedlings in containers.

See also

Asparagus beetle (page 90), Bird damage (page 91), Brassica wire stem (page 92), Cutworms (page 82), Damping off (page 81), Millipedes (page 81), Narcissus bulb fly (page 82), Rots (page 82), Vine weevil (page 83).

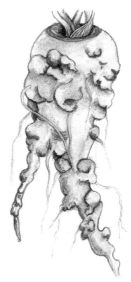

Root knot eelworm

Wart disease of potatoes

Wireworm

Season by season

Like everything else in the garden, pests and diseases are ruled by the seasons. They have active periods, when they feed and spread and can be a real nuisance, but there are also times when they're not much of a problem. One of the best ways to keep problems at arm's length is to know when they're just about to start making mischief and to take precautions against attack. There's a danger that this section could turn you into a horticultural hypochondriac. It shouldn't. It just makes you aware of what *could* be attacking your plants and *when* it is likely to be in evidence.

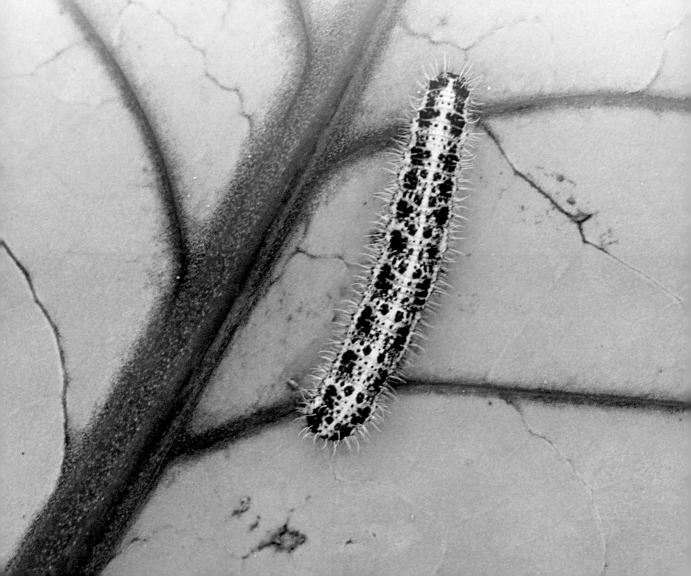

Spring

Spring is a busy time for gardeners and plants, as well as for pests and diseases. It is almost impossible to get around to all the jobs that need doing, so make a list of things you would like to achieve and set yourself sensible targets. It is much better to do a few things well, than lots of things rather badly.

Spring tasks

Plants work extra hard in spring, putting on huge amounts of growth and forming flowers too. Most come out of their winter dormancy raring to go, but they benefit from extra help in the form of food, support and general tidying-up.

Scattering slow-release fertilizer around fruit trees, ornamental shrubs and young trees is a quick job that ensures they have what they need to perform well over the coming year. Follow feeding with mulching, another quick and rewarding task that makes everything look neat and will preserve moisture around their roots. Mulching also prevents fungal spores splashing up onto new growth, so this job is particularly important if fungal infections were a problem last year.

Cast an eye over stakes and supports and replace them before they collapse. At the same time, check for early signs of insect damage and potential problems, such as dieback and cankers.

Tie in stems of sprawling climbers such as clematis, perennial pea and jasmine before they tie themselves in knots. Leave it too late and you will risk damaging the stems as you tidy them up. Again, check the plants for signs of pests or diseases as you go.

Weeding is an almost year-round task, but in spring it is doubly effective, since weeds removed now will never get the chance to set seed. Cover open, unplanted or newly dug ground with opaque plastic sheeting to prevent them germinating. While you are still in the mood for weeds, choose a still day when no rain is forecast to apply a weed-and-feed product to your lawn. Get in there early and you should soon have a healthy sward.

Clean out greenhouses, polytunnels and sheds if you didn't do this in autumn or winter. Prepare to shade greenhouses when the weather warms up.

Keep your hoe handy and do a bit of weeding every time you have a spare few minutes. Time invested now will be repaid with less work later.

Planting

Once you are on top of maintenance tasks, you can get on with the fun of adding to the garden. There is still time to plant trees, shrubs and perennials. Spring plantings must be

Don't forget

Note overcrowded clumps of daffodils and other bulbs. Once flowering is over, lift and divide them to increase flowering. Feed bulbs and let leaves fade; never cut them off.

Many plants put on a huge amount of growth in the spring and may suffer if they don't have the nutrients they need. Use a slow-release fertilizer to ensure they are well provided for, scattering it around the base of plants.

watered regularly until they are well established. In a dry year, be prepared to water trees and shrubs from now until autumn.

Seed-sowing is one of the major occupations of spring. If you have a greenhouse, polytunnel, or even just a propagator (ideally heated) and a well-lit windowsill, you can start a huge range of plants into life from seed in early spring. Make outdoor sowings in late spring. Protect all seedlings from hot sun, which easily scorches the young leaves, and

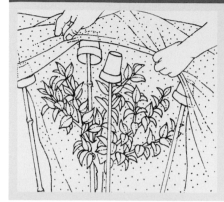

Horticultural fleece

This inexpensive, lightweight material has myriad uses. It is ideal for protecting young plants against cold nights. Early-flowering shrubs and even small fruit trees can also be covered if frost is forecast, and this gentle protection will make all the difference. Fleece is recommended for covering newly sown carrots to prevent attack by carrot fly. In some areas leeks, onions and other alliums may need similar protection against leaf miners, and it will prevent cabbage root fly reaching young brassicas, too. Where narcissus fly is a problem, cover the leaves after flowering to reduce potential damage.

If they have been raised under cover, even hardy plants need a period of adjustment, known as 'hardening off', before they can be planted out.

watch out for damping off. Wait until the weather is settled and mild before hardening off and putting your precious youngsters outdoors. Unexpected frosts combined with cold winds can cause havoc, even among more mature plants, if a mild spell has tempted them into precocious growth.

Check potted plants and cuttings and pot them on if necessary. Top-dress plants in large containers by removing the top few centimetres of compost with a trowel and replacing it with new.

Spring problems

Pests and diseases love spring too. Most pests are dormant throughout winter and wake up extremely hungry in spring. Diseases also tend to be dormant in winter and make their presence felt as plants start back into growth.

Don't forget

Now is a good time to order biological controls (see page 27), particularly those against slugs, since these are most active and harmful in the warm, damp days of mid-spring.

Early spring

Pests to watch out for include apple suckers, figwort weevils, flea beetles, leafhoppers, lily beetles and their larvae, rosemary leaf beetles, vine weevil larvae, and slugs and snails. Carrot fly and onion fly are already active in the vegetable garden. Check your soft fruit garden for signs of blackcurrant big bud mite and raspberry spur blight, both of which first become evident in early spring. As fruit trees come into bloom, keep an eye open for blossom wilt and take action as soon as possible to limit its effects.

Mid-spring

The early-spring pests are still active and they are joined in mid-spring by gooseberry sawfly larvae, which

soon defoliate gooseberry plants if not checked. Cabbage root fly becomes active around now, so protect new brassica plantings with collars or horticultural fleece. Watch out for pollen beetles when you pick spring blooms for indoor displays.

As plants grow away more strongly, diseases such as hellebore black death and fireblight become more obvious. Wherever you see signs of problems, react quickly to prevent them spreading, becoming more serious or even fatal.

As peach trees come into full leaf, remove plastic sheeting that has protected them from peach leaf curl since late winter.

Late spring

The warm, settled weather of late spring is popular with a new batch of insects, along with those that emerged earlier. Now is the time that pests such as bay and box sucker may make an appearance.

Placing a gritty barrier around plants that are often targeted by slugs and snails should help to reduce damage.

Check under the leaves of berberis for berberis sawfly larvae. Capsid bugs and caterpillars appear from now until late summer or even early autumn, as do slugworms and asparagus beetles. Check developing fruits of pears for pear midges and apples and plums for sawfly larvae. In ponds, water lily beetle larvae may damage leaves.

In damp, cool weather or humid, still weather fungal infections may develop, particularly among seedlings. Be ready to dispose of badly infected plants to avoid spread to healthy ones.

Night exercises

From mid-spring to early autumn, make forays into the garden after dark to capture vine weevils and slugs and snails. You might catch a glimpse of strawberry seed beetles too.

One of the best ways to avoid problems with insect pests is to prevent them reaching vulnerable young plants by using fine-mesh, crop-protection netting.

Summer

After the frenetic activity of spring, summer is comparatively calm. However, if spring has been wet or cold, early summer may be just as busy while you catch up on tasks you couldn't do earlier. If you have managed to keep up to date, be content to relax and enjoy the garden, while still maintaining a careful look-out for early signs of pests or diseases.

Summer tasks

Watering is among the most important of all summer gardening activities. Young plants need plenty in order to establish and grow healthily, while fruit and vegetables will not crop satisfactorily if they don't get enough. In dry periods, container plants suffer sooner than those in the ground and usually need daily watering in summer.

After watering comes feeding. Most ornamental plants do not require regular feeding. However, there are exceptions, such as clematis, which really do repay weekly or fortnightly feeds. The majority of vegetable plants are best fed as part of a weekly routine. Watch out for nutrient deficiencies (*see* page 25) in fast-growing plants and provide tonic feeds if necessary.

You should have completed most pruning by late winter, but one exception is members of the cherry family (*Prunus*). Prune these now – if necessary – since pruning wounds heal more quickly in summer, which helps them to avoid developing silver leaf disease.

Dig individual weeds out of lawns as soon as they appear to prevent spread. Use spot weedkiller if needed. During dry spells, reduce mowing and consider watering lawns to maintain grass health.

Dead-head annual flowers on a regular basis to ensure continued production of blooms. If other plants are disappointing in their flower displays, try to establish the cause and take steps to prevent a reoccurrence of the problem next year. Overfeeding (*see* box, opposite), insect pests, poor growing conditions or poor health may all be responsible.

Summer problems

Many of the insect pests that first appear in spring are still around in summer, and the hot weather may increase their numbers. Other problems can start being a nuisance in early summer, when dry, hot weather also encourages fungal diseases. Viruses often become more evident in the garden as plants settle into full growth.

Don't forget

Hardly any plant is immune to the attentions of aphids, but healthy plants are more likely to shrug off attacks. Attend to your plant's cultivational needs and try removing pests by hand before reaching for the insecticide.

Like us, plants must have adequate water in order to survive. During dry weather, even well-established specimens benefit from a good soaking.

Early summer

As the weather heats up in early summer, plants under attack from insects may show more signs of stress than they would in cooler, damper months. Thrips in particular love warm weather, and plants suffer most from their attentions during hot spells. Pea thrips can devastate pea crops. Where alder sucker and willow leaf beetle have been a problem in previous years, consider spraying against infestation now.

Gardeners, beware!

Some common problems are caused by gardeners being either overzealous or reacting too slowly or inadequately. Here are some to watch out for:

■ **Too much fertilizer** Overfeeding will produce lush, leafy growth, often at the expense of flowers or crops, and is a cause of fanging or forking in root vegetables. Overfed plants are more vulnerable to pests, such as aphids, which love soft growth.

■ **Too much water** Don't always assume that wilting is caused by drought; waterlogging has the same effect. If plants sit in water for too long, the leaves will turn yellow, the roots eventually disintegrate and plants begin to die back or die altogether. Potted plants are particularly vulnerable to overwatering.

■ **Drought** Lack of water produces symptoms very similar to waterlogging. Flowers may not develop and fruit may not form, or they drop when immature. Bolting may occur in plants such as lettuces and radishes.

■ **Erratic water supply** Heavy watering followed by periods of dryness can cause splitting in fruit and root vegetables, such as tomatoes and potatoes. Erratic water supplies may also prevent fruit from forming.

■ **Weedkiller contamination** Accidental contamination with weedkiller causes foliage to grow twisted and narrow. It often turns yellow too. Tomato plants are particularly sensitive to weedkiller.

■ **Scorching** This is a common problem in greenhouses, where water may sit on plants that are in full sun. Scorching produces pale patches on leaves; these areas then dry out and die.

Identifying aphids

If you find small, green, pink, yellow or black insects clustered under leaves or on young shoots, the chances are they will be aphids.

Greenfly

Blackfly

Early summer is often when you start to notice leaf miners cocooned inside leaves. If they offend you, squash the leaves to reduce numbers.

Cutworms start to graze on seedlings and young crops now, while the first crops of strawberries may be marred by strawberry seed beetle. Look out for apple capsid bug damage to shoot-tips and young fruit. You are too late to act this year, but if attacks are really bad, consider spraying at petal-fall next year. Continue to deal with lily beetle, slugs and snails, caterpillars, apple and plum sawfly larvae and asparagus beetle.

Red spider mite and scale insects proliferate during summer. Keep an

Unexplained wilting

If plants wilt even when well watered, one of the following may be responsible, depending on the plant type: clematis wilt (page 76); club root (page 110); cutworms (page 82); fungal wilt (page 67); onion fly (page 111); peony wilt (page 85); potato blight (page 96); primula brown core (page 82); root aphids (page 110); root knot eelworm (page 113); swift moth caterpillar (page 83); tomato blight (page 106); vine weevil (page 83).

eye out for red spider mite on greenhouse and conservatory plants, or those outdoors against sunny walls. Check under the leaves of citrus plants and remove scale insects as they appear. Black aphids attack the tops of broad bean plants (*see* above right) as well as dahlias, poppies and nasturtiums from early summer onwards. Treat them as soon as you see them.

If you plan to spray for black spot on roses, do so now, since this disease really takes hold in midsummer (*see* page 120). Watch out for rust infections developing elsewhere and remove any affected parts as soon as possible.

In the fruit garden, remove any canes of raspberries and hybrid berries showing signs of the purple cankers caused by raspberry cane spot. Watch out for American gooseberry mildew on gooseberries and blackcurrants, too. Where raspberry beetle has been a problem on loganberries, spray as the petals fall; spray blackberries as the flowers open. On raspberries, wait until the tiny fruitlets begin to turn pink.

Dead-heading is a pleasant way to spend time in the garden, enjoying the fruits of your labours and ensuring further blooms. Snip off flower stems or remove individual flowers as they fade.

Birds enjoy a range of fruit including blackcurrants. Protect them with fine-mesh netting (*see* page 117) or be prepared to lose them.

Midsummer

Don't relax your vigilance against garden pests, many of which may continue to be a nuisance from early spring until late summer. Figwort weevil, flea beetle, lily beetle and thrips are all out and about now. If you want to spray against scale insects, now is the best time, since the scale nymphs are emerging and they are more susceptible to pesticides than the adults.

Showery weather followed by bright sunshine, which is often typical of British summers, can cause rose bud balling. Remove affected buds to prevent the spread of fungal infections. While you are checking for affected buds, also cast an eye around the leaf-tips of roses against hot walls. If the weather is dry, they may be beginning to show signs of powdery mildew. Set up a regular watering routine to prevent problems from developing.

In the vegetable garden, potato blight can occur from now on. Warm, damp weather almost guarantees it in some parts of the

Tomato treatments

Take particular care of tomatoes as they flower to ensure a good crop. During dry weather, mist or shake flower trusses to avoid dry set and hollow fruit. If tomato blight has been a nuisance in previous years, consider using a copper fungicide at fruit set.

Rose problems

Two of the most common rose diseases, black spot and powdery mildew, become evident in summer. Take preventative measures to avoid them (*see* pages 86 and 88).

Black spot

Powdery mildew

country. Check for dieback in leek leaves, which may indicate white tip disease. Like many fungal infections, the sooner this is caught, the less chance you have of problems in future years. Other fungal diseases to watch out for include broad bean chocolate spot and brassica white blister, both of which are more prevalent in a damp, cool summer. If the weather is particularly hot, give celery plants some shade and feed them with a calcium supplement to prevent heart rot. Earth up carrots to avoid green top.

Get pheromone traps organized for monitoring codling moth activity towards the end of summer and watch out for early signs of birds and wasps attacking fruit. Throwing fine-mesh netting over currants and gooseberries will save at least some of your crop.

Late summer

Enjoy the warm evenings of late summer. Most insect infestations will be past their worst and if you have been carrying out damage limitation exercises since spring, nothing much should surprise you now. There are a few late-summer bad guys to look out for, such as eelworms, which seem to be at their most active in the damp days of late summer and early autumn.

If you have had problems with rhododendron lacebug, consider spraying now to prevent adults from laying eggs. It should hardly be necessary, but if you want to spray against rosemary leaf beetle, now is also a good time.

In the vegetable garden, ripening sweetcorn may show signs of

A traditional and environmentally friendly pest control, the jam-jar wasp trap is also very successful. Hang the jar filled with a sugary solution near to where you see most wasps.

sweetcorn smut, which needs to be dealt with as soon as possible. Cucumbers in greenhouses may show symptoms of powdery mildew. Pick off badly affected leaves and water plants well to keep them going until mid-autumn. Under cover, also watch out for chrysanthemum blight.

If you haven't already done so, put up some wasp traps to divert the wasps and keep numbers down, because this is when aging wasps seek out any sugary food or drinks you take outside.

Towards the end of their cropping period, most cucumbers suffer from powdery mildew. Keep an eye open for early signs as you harvest the fruit, which is not affected.

Autumn

Autumn can feel like the end of the year in the garden, but it is really the start of next year's opportunities. Assess how well your garden has performed over the year and make plans to ensure that next year is even better. You can also get on top of some of the more persistent garden problems, create new borders and beds, and plant new trees, shrubs and perennials.

Prevent damage to tender plants like citrus by bringing them under cover before the weather turns cold.

Autumn tasks

Autumn is the ideal time for planting, since the plants have the chance to produce new roots before winter. A handful of slow-release fertilizer, along with some mycorrhizal fungi (*see* page 21) in each planting hole, helps new plants to establish and grow away strongly, which is, of course, the secret of good health. Divide and replant perennials that have been showing signs of age, such as reduced flowering.

Check tree stakes and tie containerized trees to trellis or fencing to prevent them from falling over during gales. Move tender plants under cover, or protect them with horticultural fleece (*see* page 116) or thick mulch. Weed and feed and renovate lawns as necessary.

Turn the contents of your compost heap. This can be a heavy task, but it puts some air back into the mix, which produces a better end result.

Autumn is the best time to prune many shrubs and trees. A sensible pruning routine is one of the best ways to ensure they remain healthy.

Autumn problems

Although insects start to die off or disappear underground in the autumn, some hang around until quite late in the year. Vine weevils are still about, as are rosemary leaf and asparagus beetles. Cabbage root fly may still lay eggs in early autumn, and wasps will be making the most of autumn fruits, including grapes, plums and apples.

Many annuals start to succumb to powdery mildew. The lives of some can be extended with regular watering and removal of dying leaves and flowers. If you have had fungal diseases, such as black spot and botrytis, rake up and burn or otherwise dispose of fallen leaves to reduce their likelihood next year. Mulch around affected trees and shrubs to prevent spores in the soil splashing up and re-infecting the plants. Watch out for honey fungus and take immediate action if you see the fruiting bodies.

As trees lose their leaves, check supports are still firm but ties are not too tight after a year of growth.

Don't forget

Botrytis, or grey mould, thrives in cool, damp conditions. Remove any damaged growth from plants, dispose of dead plants and keep your garden tidy to reduce the chances of it causing problems.

Winter

Winter usually means spending less time in the garden. On fine days, you can nip out to pull up some last-minute weeds, do a little pruning, or check whether any buds are showing yet, but for the most part, it is a matter of preparing and planning for next year. Time spent like this is not wasted, since it allows you to get a head start in the spring.

Most pruning work can be done through winter, so you start next year with tidy, healthy trees and shrubs.

Winter tasks

Make a note of particular trouble spots and decide on preventative treatments, such as biological controls, where necessary. If you have areas where plants always seem to struggle or individual plants that regularly suffer from health problems, your options are to move them elsewhere, improve the growing conditions and/or put something else in their place.

Now is a good time to get large areas of weeds, such as brambles and nettles, under control. Choose dry weather and the roots will come up much more easily. Continue with pruning on fine days through the winter. Once leaves have fallen, cankers may become more apparent. Check trees and prune out affected branches.

If your climbing roses are regularly being affected by fungal diseases, consider replacing, cleaning or painting their supports, as these can harbour spores.

Make some time to clean out polytunnels and greenhouses and sort out the garden shed, washing pots and seed trays and stacking them neatly. It is truly wonderful to open the shed in spring and find everything ready for seed sowing.

Washing your pots at the end of the season, in warm, soapy water, will eliminate fungal spores and prevent the spread of pests and diseases.

Winter problems

Frosts in late winter can cause withered, blackened or brown leaves and young shoots. Protect early growth with horticultural fleece when cold weather is forecast.

Where the damage is due mainly to cold winds, usually only one side of the plant is affected (*see page 17*). Erecting windbreaks is one solution. Watch out for wind rock, where constant movement of the above-ground parts stops the plant rooting properly. Stake affected plants.

Cover peaches growing against walls or other structures with plastic sheeting from midwinter until late spring to protect the new leaves from peach leaf curl.

If you're spraying against adelgids, late winter is the time to do this.

Regularly check stored vegetables, bulbs, tubers and corms for rots. Dispose of those that show any signs of deterioration.

Don't forget

Get ahead and plan your spring seed planting with beneficial insects, such as bees and hoverflies, in mind.

Index

Page numbers in *italics* refer to entries in the Garden weeds and Lawn weeds galleries and Plant problems and remedies directory.

I

Iberis 110
ice plant 15
Ilex 19
Impatiens 66, 73
insects, control of 26–7, 116, 117
Iris pseudacorus 19
irises 19, 23, 71, 82
ivies *see Hedera*

J

Japanese anemone 42
Japanese knotweed 32, *38*
Japanese maples 14; *see also Acer*
Jasminum nudiflorum 19
Juglans 63
junipers (*Juniperus*) 72

K

Kalmia 80
kiwi fruit 102
knotgrass 32, *54*

L

laburnum 62
lacewings 13, 64
ladybirds 12, 13, 64, 70, 90
lady's mantle 42
Lamium maculatum 42
larch (*Larix*) 62, 80
Lathyrus 74, 85
Laurus 72
   L. nobilis 64
lavender (*Lavandula*) 19, 71
lawn sand 50, 59
lawn weeds 52–5
lawns 44–59
   diseases/pests of 56–9
   maintaining 46–9, 57
   moss in 50–1, *55*
   weeds in 46, 50–1, 52–5, 59
   wildflower 51
leaf-cutter bees *86*
leaf miners 69, 93, 116, 119
leaf problems 62–74, 90–7
leaf spots 69
leaf weevils 69
leafhoppers 69, 85, 87, 117
leatherjackets 27, *58*
leek moth 92
leek white tip 94
leeks 72, 73, 93, 94, 96, 111, 116, 121
lesser celandine 32, *39*
lettuce root aphid *110*
lettuces 11, 73, 90, 97, 110, 113
Leucothoe 80
Leyland cypress 79
lichen 56

Ligustrum 73, 79
lilac 79
lilies (*Lilium*) 70, 74
lily beetle *70*, 117, 119, 120
lime nail gall mite *63*
lime (*Tilia*) 63, 79; *see also*
   citrus trees
Limonium platyphyllum 19
Lobularia 67
loganberries 98, 103
Lonicera 15, 70, 74
Lotus corniculatus 53
low-fertility soil 19
Lunaria 92
lupins 73, 74
Lysichiton americanus 19
Lysimachia nummularia 42
Lythrum salicaria 19

M

magnesium deficiency 25
magnolias 65, 77, 80
Malcolmia maritima 19
Malus see apples; crab apples
manganese 25
maples 14, 68, 77
Matthiola 67, 109, 110
mealy bug 27, *70*
Medicago lupulina 53
Mentha 11
Michaelmas daisies 73
micronutrients 25
mildew 26, 27
   American gooseberry *90*, 119
   downy 21, *66*
   powdery 22, *70*, *88*, 120, 121, 122
mile-a-minute 42
millipedes *81*
mind-your-own-business 42
mining bees 59
mint 11
mites
   blackcurrant big bud *91*, 117
   gall *63*, *68*
   parasitic 27
   pear leaf blister *95*
   red spider 11, 17, 22, 27, *71*, 119
   tarsonemid *73*
moles 59
molybdenum 25
monkshood 66
Monstera 73
montbretias 23, 43
Morus 76
moss 50–1, *55*
mountain ash 9, 63, 68
mouse-ear chickweed *53*
mulberries 76
mulches 33, 115

mullein moth 66
Muscari armeniacum 43
mushrooms *57*
mycorrhizal fungi 21, 122
Myosotis 42

N

Narcissus see daffodils
narcissus bulb fly *82*, 116
nasturtiums 11, 64, 67, 119
nature, understanding 9–13
nectar-robbing bees *99*
nectarines 95, 102, 105
nematodes 11, 27, 67
Nepeta 11
nesting boxes 12
Neuroterus numismalis 63
newts 12
nitrogen 25
'notifiable' problems 61
nutrient deficiencies 25

O

oak 63, 80
Oenothera biennis 42
Olearia 19
onion bull neck *110–11*
onion eelworm 95
onion fly *111*, 117
onion rot *111*
onions
   bulb/root problems 82, 110–11, 113, 117
   leaf problems 72, 73, 93, 94, 95, 97, 116
ophiobolus patch *57*
orchids 74
organic methods 24, 26–7, 31, 34, 59, 90
Origanum vulgare 19, 42
ornamental plants 62–89
   flower problems 84–5
   invasive 42
   leaf problems 62–74
   pond problems 75
   root/plant base problems 82–3, 109, 110
   rose problems 86–9
   seed/cutting problems 81
   stem/bark problems 76–80
   tree leaf problems 62–3

P

pansies 69, 70
Papaver 14, 43, 119
   P. rhoeas 19, 42, 43
   P. somniferum 42
parasitic wasps 12, 27, 64, 90
parsley 93, 109
parsley-piert *52*
parsnip canker *111*

parsnips 79, 93, 95, 97, 109, 110, 111
Parthenocissus 19
patios/paving, weeding 30–4, 33
pea and bean weevil *95*
pea moth *102*
pea thrips *102–3*, 119
peach leaf curl *95*, 117, 123
peach split stone *103*
peaches 85, 99, 102, 103, 105, 116
pear leaf blister mite *95*
pear midge *103*, 117
pear scab *100*
pear stony pit virus *103*
pearlwort *55*
pears
   bark problems 76, 80
   flower problems *99*
   fruit problems 100, 102, 103, 105
   leaf problems 63, 94, 95, 97
peas 11, 70, 73, 95, 97, 102–3, 119
pelargoniums 73, 74
penstemons 67
peony wilt *85*
peppers 93, 106
perennials 15, 23
periwinkles 42, 71
Perovskia 71
pesticides 26–7, 90
pests 26
   see also under flower problems; leaf problems; rose problems; stem/bark problems; individual pests or plants
Petasites fragrans 32, *38*
petunias 74
Phalaris arundinacea 42
pheromone traps 27, 102, 121
Phlomis fruticosa 19
phlox 67, 70
phosphorus 25
phygelius 67
Phytophthora
   P. infestans 96, 106
   P. porri 94
pieris 14, 71, 80, 85
pinks 72
Pinus 62
   P. sylvestris 19
pittosporum 79
plant base/root problems 82–3, 109–13
plantain (*Plantago*) 54
planting 21, 23, 115–16, 122
plums
   bark problems 76, 79, 80
   flower problems 85, 99

Acknowledgements

BBC Books and OutHouse would like to thank the following for their assistance in preparing this book: Phil McCann for advice and guidance; Robin Whitecross for picture research; Candida Frith-Macdonald for help with illustrations; Ruth Baldwin for proofreading; June Wilkins for the index.

Picture credits

Key t = top, b = bottom, l = left, r = right, c = centre

PHOTOGRAPHS

All photographs by Jonathan Buckley (including page 17 in conjunction with National Trust Picture Library) except those listed below.

GAP Photos Pernilla Bergdahl 29l; Dave Bevan 120tr; Tim Gainey 29r; Michael King 121t; Sharon Pearson 43t; Martin Schröder 15; Juliette Wade 2–3, 13(2)

Sue Gordon 117b

Andrew McIndoe 50br, 50t, 51

Nature Photographers Ltd Richard Revels 13tl

Robin Whitecross 42, 119r

ILLUSTRATIONS

Lizzie Harper 5l, 16, 20, 21, 23, 47, 49, 56, 57, 58, 59, 62, 63, 64c & b, 65, 66t & c, 67t & b, 68, 69c & b, 70t, 70b, 71t, 71b, 72c, 73t, 74t, 75, 76t, 76c, 77, 78, 79, 81b, 83t, 86, 87, 88, 89, 90b, 93b, 97b, 101b, 106t, 110t, 113b, 116

Susan Hillier 4, 5r, 25, 35, 36, 37, 38, 39, 40, 41, 52, 53, 54, 55, 64t, 66b, 67c, 69t, 70c, 71c, 72t, 72b, 73b, 74b, 76b, 81t & c, 82, 83c & b, 84, 85, 90t & c, 91, 92, 93t & c, 94, 95, 96, 97t & c, 98, 99, 100, 101t & c, 102, 103, 104, 105, 106c & b, 107, 108, 109, 110c & b, 111, 112, 113t & c

Janet Tanner 30

Thanks are also due to the following designers and owners, whose gardens appear in the book:
Darina Allen, Ballymaloe, Co. Cork, Ireland 11; Christopher Lloyd, Great Dixter, East Sussex 9l; The National Trust, Sissinghurst Castle Gardens, Kent 17; Carol and Malcolm Skinner, Eastgrove Cottage Garden Nursery, Worcestershire 8; Sue and Wol Staines, Glen Chantry, Essex 18l; Alan Titchmarsh 10